A Chief Constable's Nightmare?

By Jeffrey Meadows QPM

Grosvenor House
Publishing Limited

All rights reserved
Copyright © Jeffrey Meadows, 2019

The right of Jeffrey Meadows to be identified as the author of this
work has been asserted in accordance with Section 78
of the Copyright, Designs and Patents Act 1988

The book cover is copyright to Jeffrey Meadows

This book is published by
Grosvenor House Publishing Ltd
Link House
140 The Broadway, Tolworth, Surrey, KT6 7HT.
www.grosvenorhousepublishing.co.uk

This book is sold subject to the conditions that it shall not, by way of
trade or otherwise, be lent, resold, hired out or otherwise circulated
without the author's or publisher's prior consent in any form of binding or
cover other than that in which it is published and
without a similar condition including this condition being imposed
on the subsequent purchaser.

A CIP record for this book
is available from the British Library

ISBN 978-1-78623-648-7

DEDICATION

To Kathleen, also known as Kathy and The Little One, for her love, support, patience and understanding over six decades.

ACKNOWLEDGEMENTS

To the readers of the draft book;
many thanks for their valuable feedback.
The Honourable Sir Richard Henriques.
Beverley and Darren Meadows
(who also helped with research at Blackpool Central
Library and the Lancashire Record Office).
Journalist David Pearce.
Solicitor and retired HM Coroner for Blackpool and Fylde,
Anne Hind.
David Williamson FCMA CGMA
(Secretary/Treasurer of the Superintendent Gerald Richardson
Memorial Youth Trust).
Ken Mackay GM QPM.

Thanks to: Trilbie Robinson, Benjamin Meadows and
Simon Smith for assisting with pagination for my book.

My thanks to:
The ladies in the Local and Family History Centre,
Blackpool Central Library.
For help readily given; Chairman Christine Pickard and
Secretary John Pickard of
Blackpool and District Branch of the National Association of
Retired Police Officers.
Peter Marlow/Magnum Photos for the use of a photograph.
Mirrorpix (Mirror Group) for use of a photograph.
Peter G. Reed for allowing use of his photographs.
Robert Stead of RS Studio, Fleetwood for permission to use
photographs from HM The Queen's visit to
the Whitewell Estate in August 1989.
The Gazette (Blackpool) for permission to use photographs;
to copy *Gazette* pages and use an extract by feature writer
Jacqui Morley.

Spot On Design and Print, Blackpool for digitalising newspaper articles and a sketch.
Former colleague David Jones for permission to use his sketches and for recreating one of them
for use in this book.
Mrs Hazel Wilkinson for permission to use two of her late husband's ink drawings.
The Chief Constable of Lancashire Constabulary for permission to use photographs, letters and published articles.

PREFACE
BY THE HONOURABLE
SIR RICHARD HENRIQUES

It gave me much pleasure to be invited to write a short introduction to this autobiography of Jeffrey Meadows. Reading it has been a pleasure. Jeffrey and I grew up in South Blackpool and much of his career in the Police Force coincided with my practising at the Bar. Whilst Jeffrey was appointed a Constable in 1957, I was called to the Bar ten years later shortly before Jeffrey's promotion to uniformed Sergeant. Many of those mentioned in this book featured prominently in my own career, in particular Judge William Openshaw, George Carman QC, Solicitors and Coroners John Budd and Sam Lee, Chief Constable Stan Parr, Superintendent Gerry Richardson, villain and artist Larry Rushton, boxer Brian London and many others.

When I was at the Bar, Jeffrey and I were both friend and foe. When together prosecuting Jeffrey was meticulous, objective and most supportive. In opposition he was combative, confident, unyielding and never overawed. He was a powerful witness with an engaging smile and a compelling delivery. Never a cross word passed between us.

Reading this book has given me immense pleasure and taken me back in time remembering Blackpool in its prime. Jeffrey recalls Blackpool's varied nightlife, mock auctions, party conferences and various public houses, all visited in the course of duty, as well as several high profile murders both in the town and the county, including the tragic murder of Judge Openshaw and the handless corpse trial in both of which Jeffrey had a prominent role.

Jeffrey, I congratulate you on a magnificent career and a most readable biography. It has been my good fortune to have featured in both.

The Honourable Sir Richard Henriques
Retired High Court Judge

September 2018

CONTRIBUTION FROM DAVID PEARCE – JOURNALIST AND LOCAL HISTORIAN

'There's a famous seaside place called Blackpool that's noted for fresh air and fun...'

So runs the famous monologue 'Albert and the Lion' written by Marriott Edgar.

But there's a lot more to Blackpool than the seafront and the Tower and the gaudy face of a world-famous holiday town.

Behind that façade is a busy town and community that manufactured aircraft and cars and much more beside and where many worked hard for their living. On its eastern edge the bricks and mortar of south Blackpool met the countryside of the Marton district once famous for the salad vegetables grown there.

And this border land was the birthplace of the man who wrote this book. He was not born with a silver spoon, but perhaps the experiences of those early days forged in him a steely strength of character and a desire to move his life forward in a positive way. He recalls the poverty but the happy times too.

Jeffrey Meadows joined the police force and learned about a darker side of Blackpool than the razzamatazz of the Golden Mile and the glitter of the Illuminations.

It was to be a long journey from those days on the beat to working major crime cases as a senior detective and then the heavy responsibility of senior management in the force.

Jeffrey Meadows tells his story in a straightforward way and it is a fascinating one which brought back many happy memories for me. As a young reporter on Blackpool's evening paper *The Gazette*

I met Jeffrey and his colleagues in the course of work and it was a memorable experience.

Later our paths crossed again through mutual friends and a shared interest in local history in which he has played no small part with honour and distinction.

David Pearce
Journalist and local historian
September 2018

INTRODUCTION

It is strange how some memories from your early life are so vivid and yet you have no recollection of other times in your life – as if events have been erased from the memory bank. Family, friends and even an old schoolmaster Bill Yates said, "You should write a book of your experiences".

"Oh yes" you say but what do you write about? What do you include and what do you leave out?"

These are the questions that exercise your mind and lead you inevitably to put off the task saying, "I'll do it sometime". Who would be interested anyway?"

The answer came from journalist David Pearce who said, "Do it, if only for the benefit of your family".

Time and time, I have made an excuse and put my thoughts to one side, but you can only prevaricate for so long! So what follows is a tale of part of my life. I would like to think it is an accurate account but in my defence, if I have strayed from the reality, it is not intentional; blame the memory. After all, I cannot be expected to get it all right – how could I? How could a chap, who according to my youngest grandson, sports an 'old farts watch' be on the ball!

It is not a diary. I do not include all that affected my life and I have deliberately omitted such things as holidays. We did not have a proper holiday until Darren was in his teens, but we have had many great holidays since. I have tended to concentrate on my working life and of course, my family life.

In the Police Service there are many things which are confidential and cannot be discussed. Incidents and cases I talk about fall into three categories; general stories; matters which are in the public domain from Court; matters which are in the public domain from publications such as newspaper reports and published books.

I have tried to contact copyright holders of photographs used in this book. In a minority of cases I have not been able to do this because some companies ceased to exist and I cannot recall who took the photograph. I sincerely apologise if I contravened any existing copyright.

I have been fortunate to have many friends and good work colleagues. You will appreciate that I cannot mention everyone and if you are not mentioned and think you should have been, I apologise.

Once, when I was a sergeant and in the thick of it, a Detective Inspector said that I was a 'Chief Constable's Nightmare,' hence the title.

It was never my intention to earn money from the publication of this book. I will not be recovering the cost of publication and printing of the book. Any income from the sale of this book, including royalties, will be divided equally between Prostate Cancer UK (Registered Charity No. 1005541 and The Superintendent Gerald Richardson Memorial Youth Trust (Registered Charity No. 504413).

CONTENTS

DEDICATION iii
ACKNOWLEDGEMENTS v
PREFACE BY THE HONOURABLE SIR RICHARD
                HENRIQUES vii
CONTRIBUTION FROM DAVID PEARCE –
                JOURNALIST AND LOCAL
                HISTORIAN ix
INTRODUCTION xi
CHAPTER 1   THE EARLY YEARS 1
CHAPTER 2   SENIOR SCHOOL 13
CHAPTER 3   TEEN YEARS 18
CHAPTER 4   MEETING KATE 24
CHAPTER 5   BECOMING A CONSTABLE 30
CHAPTER 6   ON THE BEAT 34
CHAPTER 7   JEFF BECOMES A JACK 53
CHAPTER 8   PROMOTION TO SERGEANT 100
CHAPTER 9   I'M NOW AN INSPECTOR 117
CHAPTER 10 PROMOTION TO DETECTIVE
                CHIEF INSPECTOR 133
CHAPTER 11 A CROWN ON MY SHOULDER
                AND LATER A PIP TO GO WITH IT 192
CHAPTER 12 RETIREMENT 223
CONCLUSION 244
APPENDIX A A TRIBUTE TO MY FATHER –
                JOHN MEADOWS SENIOR 248
APPENDIX B LISTINGS OF ROYAL VISITS 250

CHAPTER ONE
THE EARLY YEARS

I was born on 15 July (St Swithin's Day) in 1938. Now obviously I did not know of the legend that if it rains on that day, it will rain for 40 days and 40 nights. However, I apparently entered into the spirit of it by 'piddling' down the midwife's apron. Nurse Metcalfe (we as kids thought that she was called Madcap!) was heard to exclaim, "Well it is St Swithin's day".

When I was born, the house at 141 Penrose Avenue (later changed to 175) was occupied by Mum (Julia Hannah, born 1911) and Dad (John Meadows Snr., born 1912), elder brother Jim (who was born before Mum met Dad and who has to this day retained Mum's maiden name Horrocks) and my brother John who was 14 months older than me. In 1942 brother Patrick was born and Sister Joan arrived during the latter part of the war years. It was one of six houses in a terrace and was rented

What does one remember of their childhood? Very little I think, although some things made sufficient impression to be able to recollect quite clearly. The war years were looming and my earliest recollections are of when I was about three or four. According to Army records Dad joined the 21st Light Anti-Aircraft Regiment in September 1940 at Preston, being transferred to 212 Battery in Manchester on 30 November 1940. He was posted to India and left from Southend on 19 March 1942 joining the 70 Heavy Anti-Tank Regiment.

Dad was apparently Absent without Leave (AWOL) from 23.59 hrs on 14 February 1942 to 11.45 hours on the next day, an absence of 11 hours and 46 minutes, for which he was to forfeit one day's pay and was confined to Barracks for seven days. On his record, the unauthorised absence was shown as 11 days and 46 minutes! Is that why he got such a punishment? And why was he AWOL? The answers might be interesting. He disembarked at Madras on 11 May, a journey of almost two months.

The above dates are important because they relate to my earliest recollection. Brother John remembers the family going to North Railway Station to wave Dad off to war. I have no recollection of that. However, I do remember my Mum taking me to see my Dad when he was serving in Manchester. I would probably be three years old. I remember dark grey clouds and all these large barrage balloons held firm by long steel hawsers. It was an eerie sight for a youngster. At the barracks we went into long Nissan huts where I waited with my Mum. Then in single line soldiers appeared, all with towels tucked lengthways into the back of their shirts. It was ablution time. I do not remember any more of that visit other than we saw Dad. Why did we visit? I do not know.

Mum played her role in the war effort. I remember for a period she worked at Stansfield's Joinery on Clifton Road, opposite the Clifton Brick works (much smaller than the big brick croft across from our home in Penrose Avenue). There she helped to make ammunition boxes for the troops.

Where we lived in Penrose Avenue, Marton, we had open fields across the road and the large brick croft with iron trucks on a railway line. The trucks carried the excavated clay. There were also two great lakes. This was our playground and we often imagined ourselves to be cowboys in a landscape not too different from what we had seen at the pictures (cinema). Nearby, gypsies used to camp in their horse drawn caravans.

I was later to see neighbours Harold Leese and Harry Parr skating on the frozen ponds on the Clifton Brick Croft. I couldn't believe my eyes because as they skated, the ice began to undulate and it was like they were skating on waves, but solid waves. Harold, one of the big boys in the neighbourhood and often talked about that phenomenon.

When I was four I was collecting buttercups for Mum in an area of ground densely populated by long stemmed buttercups. What I did not know was that the thick cluster of buttercups concealed a hole where someone had removed a quantity of soil. I stepped forward and fell into the hole and fell on my left hand. Unfortunately, I fell onto a broken glass bottle which left me with a cut so deep that it seemed my hand was hanging in two halves. I ran home screaming and I was taken to Victoria Hospital where the doctor inserted one stitch! My Mum, not being too happy took me to our local doctor who put further stitches in. I have been left with a large scar, still very visible to this day. I always felt that if it had been treated properly at the hospital, the scar would not be so prominent.

Our surgery was in Penrose Avenue at the junction with St Edmunds Road. In those early days, there was no National Health Service and the 'Doctor's man' used to call every Friday night to collect one shilling per week. On many occasions Mum used to instruct us to tell the collector that she was not at home.

Going to the junior school during the war years was an experience. We went to Baines Endowed Primary School at the top end of Penrose Avenue; the posh end. We were all supplied with Mickey Mouse gas masks, so named because they were made of pink rubber with a flap at the front. The gas masks had their own box. Children had to carry them at all times together with a note giving their name and address. Many years later in the Constabulary Officer's Mess at Hutton, I was waxing lyrical about my Mickey Mouse gas mask, when as quick as a flash, a colleague Ray Rimmer said, "Well you can take it off now Jeff!", much to the amusement of those gathered in the Mess.

Where the school nursery stands today, there were underground air raid shelters. My mother used to say that when the air raid sirens sounded she could hear me running along Penrose Avenue shouting, "Mummy, Mummy".

When the sirens sounded, all the kids would go under a big table. One treat was to get dripping butties which tended to keep us quiet until the all clear sounded! We also got free school dinners.

We knocked about with some little devils. On one occasion, I was walking home with one of my friends, suddenly, without any warning he dropped his short trousers and was defecating in the middle of the pavement. I was shocked but he simply told me that if I said anything, he would tell everyone I had done it!

One of the least pleasant experiences was being taken out of school by the uniformed NSPCC Inspector. I think he was called Redfern, but I may have got that wrong. At this time Dad was in Burma and Mum had been taken into Hospital. Brother John and I were taken to the Blackpool Orphanage on Talbot Road. We went to Devonshire Road School for the month we were at the orphanage. Jim was allowed to stay at home and Brother Patrick was taken to the long gone Wood Street Mission in Squires Gate Lane, close to the railway bridge.

Ours was not a happy experience at the orphanage. The regular orphans did not like us being there and frightened us to death each night, talking about severed heads being in the large hat boxes on top of the wardrobes. I remember clearly being served with a purple coloured concoction which I took to be some form of gruel. It was awful. When we returned home, I remember Mum scolding the tall NSPCC Inspector. We had come back infected with head lice, or 'biddies' as we called them. I can hear her now saying, "We don't have much money but when you took my boys away they were clean. You've brought them back walking".

We were a poor family but we were always well fed. Mother could not afford a Christmas tree or shop bought decorations, so we made our own. Because we could not afford a Christmas tree, Mum got hold of two hoops from a barrel and made a 'mistletoe bough' which she decorated. We got sheets of coloured crepe paper and cut them into long strips, twisting them into festoons.

During the wars years presents at Christmas were rare. A neighbour, we called him 'Old Grogan', built a fort out of wood and that was the boys' Christmas present. One year as we had no presents, we were given sixpence each to buy a present. In June Avenue, there were two shops in the front rooms of terraced houses. Bobby's was one and Riley's the other. We went to Riley's shop and I bought a little bone car with the sixpence (2½ new pence). It was a great present.

There was one time when we did get a good present. The American servicemen put on a party at the Oxford Cinema for all the local kids and we all received a nice present. Mum was a friendly Cumbrian lass and we got quite a few rides on the American jeeps – but that's another story!

During the war an anti-aircraft searchlight battery was set up on the land adjoining the brick croft, opposite the Welcome Inn. Often whilst playing and crawling in the grass we would come across real soldiers on training exercises.

With brothers Jim and John on a Saturday afternoon, I would go to the 'Tuppenny Rush' at the Empire Cinema on Hawes Side Lane. We paid 2d each, hence the name. Western (cowboy) films were very popular and we used to re-enact the films as we made our way home through the brick croft. The nickname for the Empire was the 'Bug', but we liked the fact that the programme changed three times a week, whereas the Oxford Cinema programme only changed twice.

When an 'A' film was being shown you had to be with an adult. We regularly went on our own. Can you imagine the reaction today at what we did? We went up to total strangers and gave them our money and asked them to take us in! We have also been known for one to pay to get in, and then go to the emergency door and let the others sneak in. In the Empire, (or was it the Oxford) there were clocks on either side of the big screen with the words,

'Eat Cookson's Bread'. The kids had a song which they sang in unison with some gusto at each performance,

> *"Don't eat Cookson's Bread, Don't eat Cookson's Bread.*
> *No bloody wonder you fart like thunder.*
> *Don't eat Cookson's Bread."*

Two of the picture houses as we called them, had Wurlitzer organs – the Odeon and the Palladium. At the interval the organs came up out of the basement and the organist entertained.

If my handwriting is not good, (and Kathy says it isn't) I blame one of my primary school teachers – Mrs Holt. To improve my handwriting, she regularly rapped my knuckles with a ruler. The only problem was that she rapped the hand I wrote with! I do not think that helped to improve my handwriting.

We were talking about childhood memories recently. Terry, a friend and neighbour said that childhood summers seemed to go on forever. I think there's some truth in that and we did not get bored. We seemed able to fill all our time. There are many childhood memories. There was no central heating in those days and as kids you liked the ice patterns left by 'Jack Frost' on the windows. Curtains sometimes were frozen to the glass and overcoats were placed on the bed to keep us warm.

One of the kid's jobs was to cut the newspaper into neat little squares, thread string through a corner to hang at the back of the toilet door. This was our toilet paper for many years. The young today think they are trendsetters when they go 'commando', we went 'commando' through necessity. There was an outside loo, apparently, when I went to the 'thunder box' I used to sing, a practice that often drew the comment from Mrs Wynne our next door neighbour, "Oh Jeffrey's at the loo!"

Many times we had to cut cardboard soles to put into our shoes because we had holes in the soles and could not afford to have them soled at the cobblers. Mother was a great cook and baked great cakes. She was not, however, the best at patching our trousers and often we were the subject of ridicule at school. I can remember other kids saying, "Don't play with the Meadows' – they have patchy pants". This sounds a cliché, but we used to ask the better off kids if we could have their apple stumps or orange peel, when oranges became available.

When you look at family photos we were a scruffy lot. If there was any trouble in the neighbourhood the Meadows' would probably get the blame.

Generally, we had a happy childhood. As mentioned earlier, our playground was the giant brick croft. There we re-enacted scenes from western films. We made rafts to sail on the lakes. Sadly these lakes claimed at least two young lives. Health and Safety did not form any part of our risk assessments. We made tin sledges from discarded scrap and slid down the steep sides of the brick croft, heights of some 20 plus feet in some cases. After the war Felton's Scrap yard on Waterloo Road sold fuel tanks shaped like long cigars. The more adventurous cut them in half to make two canoes! We also managed to acquire old rifles with all the mechanical parts taken out and this added authenticity to our games. We played in the fields adjoining the brick croft and one Easter after we had attended Elim Church, Gracie Johnson, a farming lass, brought us painted eggs which we rolled down the hilly grassy slopes.

Elim was not the first church we went to. During our young years we attended Marton Gospel Mission, a non-denominational church run by the Taylors. We were still attending that Sunday School when Dad eventually returned from the war. Mum was christened a Roman Catholic but she must have fallen out with her church at one time. She had married Dad at St Peter's Parish Church on Lytham Road, Blackpool on 22 August 1936.

Depending on your view, you either received a good religious upbringing at Marton Gospel Mission, or you were brainwashed.

Hellfire and Damnation were never far away when Old Man Taylor preached. Of course, we didn't take it too seriously and used to love the skittish song:

"Will you come to Marton Mission, Will your Come?
Bring your own ammunition and a gun.
Old Pop Taylor will be there.
Throwing peanuts in the air.
Will you come to Marton Mission, Will you come?"

Old man Taylor didn't miss a trick. He saw us spending our collection money to buy an ice-cream, so we got reprimanded in the sermon! I think the Taylors had some sympathy with the Jesuits motto, 'Give me a child until he is seven and I will give you the man'. They certainly tried with Brother John and me. Over a period of time we had to write out verbatim, the full text of the four gospels of the New Testament. We also had to attend a weekly prayer meeting. Only two of us attended. In these Pentecostal faiths, they do not believe in praying from books. You prayed from the heart. In other words, you had to make it up as you went along. First John would start, but after a minute or two he would dry up.

"Now it's you Jeffrey," Mrs Taylor would say.

So off I went, drying up sooner than John.

"Right John, you carry on," and so it went on.

First it was John's turn, then mine. There was no remission for good behaviour! At this tender age, what did you pray about? I was looking at some prize books I won at the Mission. I was 10 years of age. They hadn't made the man by the time I reached seven. In fact, they were still trying when we left to go to Elim!

At the end of the second world war we went to a party in nearby Winton Avenue (where Harold Leese lived). It was a typical street party of that era and I can remember a piano playing man – the piano was on a cart. Of course, in those days the sight of a horse and cart was a regular thing. From the 'Rag and Bone' man to the Small Holders who sold their vegetables from their carts.

According to the *Visit Blackpool* website, at the commencement of the Second World War Blackpool received some 37,500 evacuees. We even had two of those. Two young sisters came to stay with us but I do not have too much recollection of their stay.

Dad came home from Burma being demobbed on 9 May 1946. He had been overseas for three years. He was virtually a stranger and I would be two months away from my eighth birthday. He had his demob suit, but his health was never good.

He had qualified as a cook at the Indian Army School of Cookery. So he went to work at the large Co-op Bakery at the junction of Preston New Road and Cherry Tree Road North (where McDonalds now stands). Dad was often off sick and on more than one occasion I had to go and tell the foreman (who to a young lad looked a fearsome character) that Dad was too ill to go to work. My memory is that the foreman was not too sympathetic. Dad also worked at Derbyshire's Bakery for a time. His bike was a carrier bike type with a square short frame at the front for a basket. It would normally be used for delivering shop orders.

I remember that we had to meet him one afternoon after he had finished work. We met him at the rear of the Old Police Station in South King Street. We all went into this room. It was full of new clothing and it transpired that we were to get free clothing from the Chief Constable's Poor Children's Clothing Fund. It was like walking into Ali Baba's cave. Racks full of new clothes causing your mind to boggle. How could this place have all these clothes and it was not a shop? I saw a jacket which was similar to an old well-worn one that I had.

"Look Dad", I proclaimed, "It's just like mine," whereupon I received a sharp retort from my Dad to "Keep your mouth shut" or I would get a 'lander'. (That's a smack round the ears!)

It was only as I grew older and wiser that I realised that when my Dad made that remark, he was frightened to death some official would have heard it and we would not need new clothes. Mum used to get what were called Provident Cheques which you paid back weekly and which were accepted at some, but not all, clothes retailers. We learned that to our cost. Mother took us to a shop on Central Drive, Blackpool and we all got decked out. It was only when she handed over the 'cheque' that the shopkeeper said that their establishment did not take that type of cheque. Talk about embarrassing as all the gear had to be put back in stock. We did find the correct shop, it was next door!

To save money, Dad put all the boys into clogs. He would then buy irons from Clegg's on Central Drive and periodically would re-iron the clogs. People could certainly hear us coming and you could get a good shine on the clogs. Another money saving idea of Dad's turned out to be a painful experience for the boys. He bought a pair of Burman hand clippers from Woolworths. He decided that he would cut the boys' hair. That was fine but he often got the clippers stuck in the hair and then tried to release it. We would give a howl of pain, only to be told, "Keep your bloody head still or you'll get a lander!"

Money was always a problem and this was the cause of many rows, sometimes heated, between Mum and Dad. In our younger days, he ruled us with a fear that never manifested into physical violence although I once saw him slap Mum quite hard during one of their rows.

This may be the reason why, on one occasion when I was very young, Mum decided she was leaving Dad and was taking Jim with her. I wanted to go with them, and although (I reckon for the right reasons) she didn't want to take me with them, she relented. We went to the Blackpool South Railway Station and then we went to the open air market behind the old Dog and Partridge Inn where she bought some cherries. Whether it was because I was with them or for some other reason, Mum changed her mind and returned home.

Jim, our big brother had been born before Mum met Dad and we could never understand why Dad never changed Jim's surname to Meadows. Although we have always regarded Jim as our full brother, his surname was Horrocks, this being Mum's maiden name.

Of course, after the war everything was on ration. How Mum fed us all, I will never know, she was not a good manager with money but she was a good manager with what food she bought. She did not particularly like housework and washing (but who could blame her having to do the weekly wash in the bath by hand!). She was however a very good cook and baker, she had come down from Whitehaven in Cumberland to go into service. She went initially in service to a family from Poulton-le-Fylde (It may have been the Watson family). We always knew how to use knives and forks and if presented with a full set of eating implements for more than one course, it was simple; 'work from the outside in'.

Even fuel for the fire was rationed and many was the time that we had to take a pram to the Gas Works (next to the Tesco Extra at Marton) for it to be filled with coke. There was no coal at that time. Kathy (my wife) had it worse. We lived in Marton, but she had to walk from Layton and back!

The outside toilet often froze up and we had to take buckets of water from the kitchen to 'flush the loo'. In the winter of 1947, I was nine years old, I recall opening the back door to a solid wall of snow which was higher than the top of the back door. We had to dig out to get to the toilet. It was hardly digging for victory! When potatoes were scarce, we had to walk to a vegetable store close to Blackpool South Railway Station. We took the trusty old pram to get as many spuds as we were allowed. We couldn't take the tram for this task, because of course, that cost money.

Fancy holidays were not on the agenda. I remember my Mum taking us to Whitehaven to see little Granddad Patrick Horrocks, a former miner at the Haig Pit and First World War cavalry man. I can still smell the tobacco from his pipe and he would tell Grandma

Elizabeth (his second wife), "Get these Laal lads a bit of cyak" ("Get these little lads a piece of cake"). We went into the town centre one morning and went into a café where Mum met one of her old boyfriends. It was strange for us kids to see this grown man holding her hand across a table and weeping, probably for a lost love.

Our relatives came for their holidays to Blackpool and where did they stay? No prizes for guessing, our house! How did we fit them all in? We went to an exotic place for a holiday called Accrington! We stayed at Auntie Agnes and Uncle Tom's in Manor Street. Cousins Bernard, Melvyn and Patricia lived there. They had outside tippler toilets. Auntie Agnes was a lovely lady. There was no seaside here, but what they had was the Coppice, latterly described on the council website as, 'The Coppice area is excellent for brisk, variable terrain walking for leisure and health enjoyment'. We kids just liked to walk along the cobbled streets and get to the top of this countryside hilly area.

One experience I learned early was about what job to get after school and at weekends. Brother John had a paper round and I sometimes went out with him. One Sunday morning, it had been raining, we were delivering the morning paper and I had been given one to deliver. I fell off my bike in Bambers Lane, Marton onto the wet pinky coloured cinder track. What a mess the newspaper was in.

"What should I do John"? I asked.

"I'll show you" he said, whereupon he took the rain sodden and torn newspaper, folded it carefully and said, "Go and put that through the letterbox", which, of course I did.

It was experiences like that and the fact that I did not want to get up early every morning and commit my time after school each day, which convinced me that this was not the job I wanted. Instead, I went for being a Butcher's Delivery Boy which only meant one evening per week and Saturday morning. Now I had some experiences doing that job, but they are for a later chapter.

CHAPTER TWO
SENIOR SCHOOL

Even though not regarded as teenage years, leaving the junior school and going to what was a secondary modern school is an introduction to your teens. None of the boys in my family passed their eleven plus examinations and like brothers Jim and John before me, I went to Highfield Secondary Modern School. The Highfield School of my days was very different to the Highfield Leadership Academy of today.

There was a boys' school with Mr Charnley as Headmaster, later succeeded by Mr Ford and a girls' school headed by Miss Hadfield and later Miss Bloomer, the boys and girls were kept separate. On the east side of the school, once occupied by the uninspiring grey sports hall was the market garden; a huge plot of land gave an opportunity for young lads to practice a form of agriculture. Gardening lessons were part of the curriculum, there was even a full-time gardener, Mr Buckley. You were often judged by the amount of weeds collected, one day one lad tried to grab some of my weeds. My natural reaction was to prevent this 'theft' by spearing the weeds into the ground with my garden fork. Unfortunately, I speared his hand to the ground. That incident passed by being regarded as 'an accident'.

Generally speaking, schooldays were relatively happy days. I was in an 'A' stream and the form master was Mr H.V. Coopey, a serious but decent man. We had an Art teacher, Bill Yates. (Bill served on the battle cruiser *HMS Hood* during the Second World War. In May 1941 *HMS Hood* along with the battleship *HMS Prince of Wales* engaged with the German battleship *Bismarck* and the heavy cruiser *Prinz Eugen*. *Hood* was struck by several German shells and exploded and sank with 1,418 men aboard, of whom only three survived. Fortunately for Bill he had left the ship earlier to go on a course, therefore he was not on board when it got sunk). Bill was a great character who also taught French. He would sometimes get his violin out and promised to play it. But like the American comedian Jack Benny, he would put it to his chin but never actually gave us a tune!

He also taught drama and he once produced a Chinese play called *'The Stolen Prince'*. There was a schools' festival and we went to Stanley Junior School to perform. I played the part of 'The Chorus'. I was, in fact the narrator and stood at the side of the stage telling the story. At one time the 'property man' started to 'roll up the river' before he should have done. I had to think on my feet and strolled across, slapped him (heavier than I had intended) and called him a silly man. It seemed to go down rather well. In the booklet produced for the school's 50th anniversary, Bill Yates referred to that play.

In July 1997, together with Kathy I was invited to Bill Yates' home. Bill then in his eighties, assisted by his daughter had been baking, and served us with a tasty collection of cakes. He had also invited some of his old colleagues and it was delightful to meet up with former PE teacher Rex Breeze and Science teacher Ted Marsh again. There were other retired teachers there and I was privileged to be the only pupil. That occasion was repeated some time later.

I had met Bill earlier when I gave a talk to the Poulton Probus Club. He had been invited as a guest by former Highfield teacher Tom Mayhew, later to become Headteacher of Revoe Primary and Junior School. It was following that talk that Bill Yates encouraged me to write my memoirs. He offered to help but sadly before I got round to it, he had passed away, but in the introduction to my book I acknowledge Bill's encouragement.

My old school was later renamed Highfield Humanities College, eventually becoming Highfield Leadership Academy. Your past can always catch up with you. On Thursday, 30 November 2017; President Eric Hind of Blackpool South Rotary Club and

I were invited to Highfield Leadership Academy's formal GCSE Senior Awards Evening and Academic Excellence and Progress Awards at the Village Hotel, Blackpool. There was a light hearted moment when the Executive Principal Mrs Helen McKenzie OBE, who had been examining the school archives, showed all present an autograph book and revealed it belonged to a certain Jeffrey Meadows. I had loaned the book along with some other items to the school some years ago.

The book brought back some nice memories. Bill Yates had written these words in French, *'Sois sage Môn vieux. Prend garde a ne pas gagner une tête trop grande',* which I believe loosely, translated means, 'Be good old man. Take care not to win a head too big". Very Sound Advice

In my day, there were certainly some characters on the teaching staff. You did not mess the metalwork teacher about. If you said that you wanted to go to the toilet, Mr 'Ding Dong' Bell would hand you an empty milk bottle! We had two teachers who sold ice cream etc., during the lunch break.

I was never proficient at sport. I even got stuck squeezing through the long school benches in an obstacle race. The sports master Mr Breeze tried to encourage the pupils. He decided that I might make a good boxer, so he put me in the ring with the school champ, George Diggle. I must say, I was doing OK and seemed to have the upper hand until Mr Breeze stopped the contest saying, "Now can we box to the Marquess of Queensbury Rules!" That was not a good move. George then started to punch me to kingdom come! However, it helped me to make a decision which was that boxing was not for me, I was content with how my face looked and did not want it rearranged by some pugilist.

Some teachers were keen on administering forms of corporal punishment. Mr Bollington was quite adept with the cane – a very strict disciplinarian. He once caned some of the dinner monitors because we had not kept the diners quiet enough. He did breed some resentment which manifested itself one day in what might be described as a reciprocal act of violence. He was stood in front of the blackboard when a missile thudded against the blackboard narrowly missing Mr Bollington's head. The missile turned out to be a rather solid kohlrabi. Had the fancy cabbage hit Mr Bollington's head, he would certainly have known about it.

Whilst Bollington kept to the traditional method of caning, old Shorrocks was not so constrained. His favourite saying was that if we misbehaved he would be 'tapping a few clarets', an old English saying for giving someone a bloody nose! He was in full flow one day and he hit this lad with a ruler, then a pencil box and finally a blow to his nose, leaving the lad with a bloody nose. Some teachers certainly got away with it in those days.

One legend at Highfield was Mr Harry Pearson, he was the Deputy Head. He was a fair minded teacher but brooked no nonsense. I was selected to become a prefect. At a school assembly when Mr Pearson was about to administer punishment to an individual, he would give me the keys for his storeroom and tell me to fetch a cane. In that storeroom, as well as all the stationery and pencils and other equipment; he kept a collection of canes. I would go in there and ponder as to which cane would inflict less pain? It was a waste of time, because whichever one I gave him seemed to have the same effect on pupils – pain and gasps!

Prefects were allowed to give minor punishments to pupils who offended against the school rules e.g. lateness. The attitude of some of the pupils was derisory. It was no real hardship to write out 'I must not be late' 25 times. Nevertheless, it could cause resentment.

I left school at the end of one term only to be set upon by some of the more unruly and bullying pupils. It is fair to say that I was 'beaten up'. It was obviously an attempt to deter me from carrying out my duties as a prefect. I was not prepared to let this happen. I spoke to Mr Coopey and said that some pupils ridiculed the '25 line system'. I suggested that we should still give 25 lines but make any offender write 25 lines in the form of an essay. Mr Coopey agreed. I will never forget how the smirk on one lad's face disappeared when I said, "25 lines as an essay on 'How the moon controls the tide'!" It was interesting that as a young policeman I had to deal with some of the lads who caused trouble at school.

I enjoyed participating in the school drama productions. However, I was never able to attend school camps or other school holidays. I managed to go on one day trip to Chatsworth House in Derbyshire and I had to save up for many weeks to go on that.

As I said earlier, my time at Highfield was good but I experienced disappointment when I was thirteen. The Headmaster Mr Ford and Mr Coopey and other staff, felt I should take the 13 plus examination to go to grammar school. Members of the teaching staff were confident that I could pass this exam. I went home elated. However, my joy was short lived. My Dad told me to forget that idea. I would be leaving school when I was fifteen to get a job like my brothers. I was disappointed and it was only in later years when I had fully matured that I realised that my Dad's priority was to 'put food on the table'.

I left Highfield in the summer of 1953. The only certificate I had was one which certified that I could leave school legally.

CHAPTER THREE

TEEN YEARS

When I left school, I started working for the Co-operative Butchery Department, being sent to the Harrowside Branch. My manager was Alwyn Greenwood whose family were builders and the first hand (assistant manager) was Tom Russell. They were good to work with and I enjoyed working there.

There was a Co-op Grocers next door and there was great friendship between the various colleagues. Ted Chadwick was the Grocery manager and he was a pleasant man.

I started to learn the trade but my main task was as a delivery boy. I was provided with a carrier bike with a very large basket and a small front wheel. We supplied private customers as well as some large hotels and smaller boarding houses.

After about a year, I decided that I could get more experience with a local butcher. I left the Co-op and went working for Reggie Fletcher who had a shop at the corner of Newhouse Road and Cherry Tree Road North, Blackpool. I had been a delivery boy there when I was at school, working Tuesday evenings and on Saturday. The shop manager was called Harry Daley and he was a great character. Reggie could be quite unpleasant, he was an old fattish man with only one eye. He had a chair on the customer side of the counter and would speak to the customers.

Mrs Fletcher however was a most delightful and gentle lady. Reggie could be mean and the delivery bike was very old fashion, it had a carrier on but it was not a purpose built delivery cycle. It was quite unstable and one day when cycling along Lytham Road, the wheels got caught in the tram lines and off I came!

I did learn with Harry – he made the shop's own sausage and brawn etc. When you were boning such things as a neck of beef (not easy to bone) or trimming meat of a beast's head, 'old Fletcher', as I called him, used to feel the bone to see if you had left any meat on! One day he was irritable and told me to be careful where I walked. I asked why and he said that he lost his glass eye. The trouble was we used to scatter sawdust on the floor to soak up blood etc., and his eye was amongst this lot! I did find it so he was able to clean it and put it back in his eye socket.

I got a lot of scratches on my hand from dressing and cleaning out chickens etc., and the scratches became infected. I was told by the doctor not to handle meat, however, they did not know Reggie, he had me working in the back shop out of sight of the customers.

I delivered meat to Sayner's Garage on Preston New Road. The owner's bungalow was at the rear of the garage, I knocked on the door, it was opened and I saw this big grey blur flying towards me, before being bitten by this savage Alsatian. I refused to continue delivering to that address.

One day, 'old Fletcher' was having a go at me and was being quite nasty. Unfortunately for him, he had not seen Mum walk into the shop.

"Get your coat Jeffrey – you're not staying here," she said, or words to that effect.

Then she had a go at Reggie. He apologised and I did go back but things did not work out as I had hoped, so I decided to leave.

I left with mixed feelings because I really liked Harry, and Mrs Fletcher had been so kind. In later years, Mrs Fletcher and my old Deputy Head, Harry Pearson were my two referees when I was joining the police.

Now I needed to get back to the Co-op, so I telephoned the Butchery Department Deputy General Manager, Mr McGuire. I told him I would like to return to the Co-op. He said he would ring me back, which he did after a few minutes, having checked with my old manager. He told me that I could start back on the following Monday.

I was delighted to learn that I was going back to Harrowside. The only thing was that it was on a hill and when the wind was blowing from the Irish Sea it took some pedalling to get over the brow! We used to load the basket up and on more than one occasion the weight tipped the bike up.

It was good to be back at Harrowside and I had some very good customers. Every Thursday I would take the invoices out to the hoteliers and I would get a nice 'dropper' from some (That is a tip). As I progressed, I would prepare the orders and I could collect as much as £250 in a week, and this was the mid-fifties.

Working for the Co-op, we had to attend educational classes at the main Emporium. One worthy who gave us lessons on the Co-op was Mr Shackleton, whose name was on a large plaque in the Coop Emporium on Coronation Street. We also attended the Park Road Annexe of the Blackpool Technical College studying for the National Meat Diploma.

We also attended the abattoir, one of the skills we learned was how to skin a sheep and we saw the slaughter men dropping bullocks, using the Cash captive bolt pistol. We also went to the Midlands to visit the large Marsh and Baxter factory, where they electro-shocked the pigs prior to bleeding them. They were large producers of ham joints and employed one man whose only job was to stick a probe into the ham and smell the probe. He decided whether the ham was fit to be sold.

A group of us sat the National Meat Diploma examination. Of that group of about a dozen lads, only one lad, Lyndon Wilson, passed. He had been a pupil at Arnold Public School. A science paper had been included in the examination and that subject had never been included in the syllabus! Can you imagine the fuss today if that happened? All my friends re-took the examination the following year and passed. I did not re-sit the examination because I was then joining the police.

I had several amusing and some not amusing experiences when butchering. I was returning to the shop one day free-wheeling my bicycle down the hill, as I approached the shop, I applied the brakes but nothing happened. I made a snap decision, and headed for the shop doorway and straight into the shop. I managed to stop but not before I had scattered a few customers!

In my day, the abattoir would supply full forequarters and hind quarters of beef. We had to carry them into the shop and it was a very wide pavement outside the shop. One day, I must have had my feet in the wrong position. I put the large hind quarter onto my shoulder and turned. I tried to walk forward but was wrong footed and fell over. I was not hurt but was so embarrassed! It was though the world was watching me.

Once a small child in a pram shouted, "Daddy," pointing at us stood behind the counter.

As quick as a flash, Alwyn the manager pointed at me and said, "Sam is the one who delivers at your house". For some strange reason, all the errand lads at this shop got christened Sam.

One lady wanted some sausage delivering and said she would be out. She said I could pop them through the letterbox. I did so, but what she had not told me was that she had a dog who very quickly consumed the sausage! People used to buy a sheep's heads for their dogs. We had to skin them, remove the eyes and then split the head in half ready for cooking. I was told to prepare a sheep's head, when it came to splitting it, I placed it in the middle of the large block table and drew the cleaver down. Unfortunately,

I struck it in the wrong place and it shot off the block straight into a lady's basket.

Perhaps my most embarrassing moment was when I was delivering a joint of beef to a lady in Woodstock Gardens. The lady lived alone but rented out rooms upstairs to showgirls. I should have guessed that there was something amiss because the two showgirls were at the window having a giggle. I knocked and the lady of the house came to the door. She was wearing a candlewick dressing gown and she had clearly been at the gin bottle.

She looked at me and said, "If I was young and beautiful I would say to you, I'm naked, I'm naked," whereupon she flung open her dressing gown. She was naked so I thrust the joint into her hand and said, "I'm off"!

Customers could be very different. We had one lady who would wait till we had cleaned the mincing machine, then buy fillet steak and have it minced for her dog. We weighed meat with the scales which had individual weights. The same lady asked if we had allowed for the thin white paper on which the meat was placed. To make her happy, the manager put a similar sized piece of paper on the part of the scale with the individual weights.

Favoured customers would receive special treatment when it came to the Co-op's famous dividend (divvy) pay-out day. The divvy would be paid out in the hall on the first floor. The favoured customers would bring in several sheets, which contained all the thin narrow dividend receipts which they stuck on foolscap size sheets. One sheet could have dozens of these small gummed receipts. Every time they shopped in a Co-op store they got a divvy receipt for the amount they had spent. And I got the job of adding up all the receipts to get a grand total for each foolscap size sheet.

I was quite naive. One of the customers was a really good looking young woman with a great figure. I heard Alwyn and Tom discussing her and Alwyn said, "I bet her husband gives her quite a thrashing".

I asked, "Why does he beat her"?

They both laughed and the comment was, "You've got a lot to learn Sam".

I was quite proficient by the time I left the Co-op and of course I had learned the odd trick of the trade. We had a large water boiler in the backyard which was always on the boil. If the black puddings had not sold within a couple of days I would put them on a big hook, immerse them fully into the boiling water. They came out steaming and went in the window. They soon sold and of course, would be fine to enjoy. If a chicken was a little pigeon-chested, scissors were inserted in from the neck end and the breast bone just clipped. It then had a nice round full breast! And a little dabbing with white flour took away any greying. The worst job was at Christmas time, dressing and cleaning the Turkeys. You always came away with many scratches on your hands and you could not get away from the smell.

I was lucky to work with good people at the Co-op. Tom Russell, an avid Blackpool Football team supporter, moved on to manage the butchery department at British Home Stores. We had two more first hands whilst I was there, Jack a Dunkirk veteran and Wilf Gosling.

I had at one time thought of studying to become a Food Inspector but I had always wanted to be a Bobby. So the decision was made to leave butchering. I spoke to the Deputy General Manager Mr McGuire and explained what I wanted to do. He was a good man. He said that he thought I was doing the right thing. Moreover, he told me that if it did not work out for me in the police, I should contact him personally and I would be welcomed back.

I did join the police but that is for a later chapter.

CHAPTER FOUR

MEETING KATE

You could say that religion brought Kathleen and me together. I had better explain that when I first met her, her family called her Kate, particularly her granddad. When I learned she was actually christened Kathleen, I thought it was a nice name and I started to call her Kathleen. Over the years friends have called her Kathleen, Kath and more recently Kathy. Friends also call her by my nickname for her, 'The Little One'. For the purposes of this story I will call her Kathy.

I met Kathy at Elim Pentecostal Church. She had been brought to the church by her friend Marjorie Warren. She was a beautiful, petite lass and I supposed I fancied her from the start. She was only sixteen. I did not feel that she would be interested in me. This was a girl who had several young lads vying for her affections!

I have to point out that at this time I was very involved with the church. I was a Sunday School Teacher and Treasurer. It is fair to say that I was a committed born-again Christian. Kathy was not. In fact she often reminds me that I told her that I wanted her to 'get saved' because I was going to heaven and she would go to hell! How things change, Kathy is the one who without fail says her prayers every night and she is a member of Marton United Reformed Church.

I usually go once a year at Christmas. I particularly liked the music which the minister Reverend Chris Weddle chose for the carol *'While shepherds watched their flocks by night'*. It was the tune for *On Ilkla Moor Baht 'at*. Sadly Chris died on 2 July 2011. He was 56 years of age. He was married to Heather and they had two children Clare and Peter. When he died, Clare was 28 and Peter 26 years old. Chris was very popular and introduced Pizza Praise to encourage youngsters to attend church.

I first met Chris at a social to welcome him when he came to Marton United Reformed Church in 1987. I was 'volunteered' to challenge him to see who could eat a bowl of trifle without hands. I won and as he raised his head from the bowl smiling, his beard was full of cream. I thought this lad will do for me.

The last time I saw him was two weeks before his death. It was at the Summer Fair. He was sat outside in the stocks. You had to pay to throw a wet sponge at him. I told him that providing we could have the *On Ilkla Moor Baht 'at* tune at the Christmas Carol Service, I would make sure that none of my sponges hit his face. With a big smile on his face he readily agreed. I think that when Chris died, the Church lost some of its soul.

People who know me now would never believe it, but I was very shy. Although I really fancied Kathy I could never pluck up the courage to ask her for a date. It was my Mum who sorted that out. We were outside church and Kathy asked me if I would give her a ride home on my bike. I said that I couldn't, whereupon Mum immediately said words to the effect, "What's up with you, you're pining all week for her".

So I agreed and she sat on my cycle crossbar. We had just passed the Welcome Inn when we were stopped by a policeman! We said we were sorry and he very kindly gave us a reprimand. I then walked Kathy home to her house in Loftos Avenue. That was the start of our courtship.

Kathy lived with her Mum Lucy, a widow, her Granddad Thomas and brother Brian and sister Rose. Kathy was the eldest and was the little big sister. Lucy worked as a waitress so was often required to work unsocial hours. Rose was 12 and Brian 13 going on 14. Much of the domestic work was left to Kathy and she had to look after her younger siblings. Old Tom was quite a character, he liked a bet and of course, at that time it was illegal. There was one occasion when he was taken away in the Black Maria. He would often buy himself some barm cakes and make a sandwich at about 4pm. When Lucy came home from work she would ask if he had eaten and invariably he said 'No'.

Tom used to argue with the television, particularly when there was a time check. He would say that the TV had got the time wrong. He had an old pocket watch which he would continually wind up as if the spring had broken. He loved the ITV show *'Take Your Pick'* hosted by Michael Miles. He thought Miles was a wonderful man to give away all the prize money. He really believed Miles was giving away his own money!

Kathy was actually two timing me and had been going out with a sailor boy who came looking for her when he was on leave. He called at Loftos Avenue only to be chased off by Tom. He was not the only boyfriend Granddad Tom chased off. Tom once said to me, "You should get a gold clock if you marry Kate".

My first meal at Loftos Avenue was quite an experience. Kathy had cooked a nice Sunday lunch and during the meal I momentarily put my knife and fork down, as you do. With the speed of lightning, Rose whipped my plate away and shared the food on my plate between Brian and her.

I was romantic and I would say to Kathy, "I love you".

Her reply was, "I do too". She could wind me up. Instead of saying, "I am not", she would say, "I aren't".

I got so exasperated one day I meant to say, "It is not I aren't, it is I am not", but I said, "It is not I aren't, it is you am not"! These lasses can get you in a tizzy.

Kathy worked as a junior at the furriers Swears and Wells in Clifton Street, Blackpool. She worked there on leaving Claremont School. She was well-thought-of at the furriers and left after three years, principally to earn more money. When she visited the shop some three weeks after she he had left, she learned that Mrs Wright, the manageress had held her job open in case she wanted to return.

When she worked there I got a letter from her saying arrangements for a meeting had been changed. The letter gives a little insight into her temperament. Note the reference to not sulking!

What surprised me was that Kathy was the sensible one of the children, but seemed to be subject to more restrictions. Brian had some dodgy friends and Rose was going out with Terry from 14 years of age, getting engaged at 16 and married at 17 years of age. Kathy had to be in at 11pm even when engaged and Tom would not go to bed till she was home and I had gone. Kathy reminds me that I made her bury gifts from former boyfriends in the back garden. Strangely, I have no recollection of that episode!

I was thinking about joining the police which Kathy fully supported. Having not long turned 18, I wrote to the Chief Constable of Blackpool Borough Police indicating my interest. I received a letter dated 31 August 1956 from the Chief Constable Mr Harry Barnes, advising me to call in at the Central Police Office on the first or second September to see Inspector Rutherford. I went and had an interview with the Inspector. He was a large, powerfully built, soft spoken Scot. It was agreed that I should complete my National Service first. I knew that I would be called soon for National Service and my plan was that after my two compulsory years, I would return to civilian life and join the police.

Robert Burns in his poem *To a Mouse*, (1786) wrote, *"The best laid schemes o' mice an' men gang aft a-gley, (often go awry)"*. I certainly had personal experience of that.

On Tuesday 29 January 1957, I travelled to Preston, my travelling companion was a school mate. He had often missed school through sickness, as he suffered from several complaints not least bronchial type complaints. On the train we were discussing our future. He and I felt that he would not be accepted for National Service because of his medical history. I would do my two years then join the police. How we were both proved wrong.

The system was that there were several specialist doctors. One checked ears, another the heart and chest. One did the 'cough' test where he felt your testicles and you had to cough. I heard a Scottish doctor who was obviously irritated saying to the lad who had come with me, "Cough man!"

When you had been seen by all the doctors, you were then checked by the Chairman of the Panel. He checked my ears and called the ear doctor. They checked my ears again and the next thing I knew, I was being told I was medically unfit for National Service and was given a card grading me as three. The next day they sent me a letter saying that men placed in Medical Grade III and IV by the Medical Boards under the National Service Acts are not regarded as available for call-up under the Acts. And my old school mate – he was accepted!

I had previously had an X-ray on 11 January 1957 and I received a letter dated 29 January (the day of my examination) advising me that 'the condition of my chest needed further investigation'. I was advised to contact my doctor.

Obviously, being rejected for the Armed Services was a great concern in view of my intention to join the police. I quickly visited my doctor who made arrangements for another X-ray and referred me to an ear consultant at Blackpool Victoria Hospital.

As far as the concern over my chest, that was soon resolved. I recalled that at the 11 January X-ray, I had giggled when the cold plate made contact which may chest. I had obviously moved and the second X-ray revealed no reason for concern.

I attended the hospital and was seen by the ear consultant and his colleague. They carried out a thorough examination and they said that there was not even any sign of a dry perforation of the ear. They concluded there was no problem with my ears. I rather naively enquired whether I should inform the Army. The consultant looked at me and told me that I should consider myself a lucky young man who did not have to undertake National Service.

The plan was still to try and join the police so I decided to brush up my Maths and English and I went to enrol at the Technical College in Palatine Road. I cycled there but when I was asked to pay the tuition fee of one shilling, I found that I had only 11½d. I was a half an old penny short. So they would not let me enrol. I cycled home and asked my dad to loan me the halfpenny, which he did. I then cycled back to the Technical College and enrolled. Dad felt I should not try to join the police. When I told him of my intention, he was far from encouraging and said, "Don't bother, you'll never get further than the Co-op".

Some years later when I was established in the police force, my brother Jim and I were trying to get Dad up the steep staircase at our home in Penrose Avenue. Dad had been out and had a few pints. He was quite drunk. It was a narrow staircase and we would get him to near the top, then he would slide down. We did get him upstairs and as we were trying he looked at me and said, "I'm proud of you Jeff". There is a phrase *in vino veritas*. I am sure that was true with Dad that night.

CHAPTER FIVE
BECOMING A CONSTABLE

I applied to join Blackpool County Borough Police. At 10am on Wednesday 11 September 1957, I attended at the Central Police Office, South King Street, Blackpool, for 'educational and medical examination and interview'. As soon as the educational examination was completed it was checked and marked. I was successful, so off I went to see Dr Bruce at his premises in Raikes Parade, Blackpool. He gave me a thorough medical examination. However, when it came to checking my ears the batteries failed in his otoscope. He told me to go to the far end of the room and he went to the opposite corner. He then whispered some words. Fortunately, it was rather a loud whisper and I was able to hear and repeat what he said and I passed the medical.

The next part of the interview process was an interview with the legendary Chief Constable, Harry Barnes. I went into his office and he appeared to be a small man and he had a bald head. Harry Barnes did not waste words.

"Why should I employ a local lad?" he asked.

"What would you do if a friend or member of your family committed an offence?"

To which I answered, "You cannot let personal feeling come into it. You must take the appropriate action".

He said words to the effect that he would take a chance and appoint me as a constable. After thanking him, I turned and started to walk out.

He shouted, "Meadows". I stopped in my tracks, turned and he rasped, "Remember, I can sack you whenever I feel like it".

Such was my welcome to Blackpool County Borough Police Force.

Just over three weeks after my interview I was appointed a constable in Blackpool County Borough Police. On Saturday, 5 October 1957, four young constables in full uniform, Mike Wrench, Tony Cross, Peter Bentham and Jeffrey Meadows were sworn in having made a solemn and sincere declaration before Mr William Pomfret, a Justice having jurisdiction in the Borough.

We were issued with brand new numbers from 188 to 191. The local Police Federation even commented on this in their newsletter. Constables and sergeants had numbers, officers did not. Mike, Tony and I served our full-time with the police. Mike was a member of Special Branch and Tony eventually became the Coroner's Officer. Peter Bentham only served for a short time.

Following the swearing ceremony, we went out on patrol in Blackpool Town Centre. We were in company of an experienced constable, until that is, they left us to go for their refreshment break. So for one hour we were left on our own, in full uniform and in the centre of Blackpool's main shopping area. People would say, "Excuse me officer" and you would not realise they were addressing you!

One lady approached Tony Cross and asked, "Can you tell me where they sell bread".

Tony was up to the mark and immediately responded, "From a bread shop". I know we were all relieved when our experienced constables rejoined us.

We had the Sunday off, then on the Monday the four of us were travelling to the No 1 District Training Centre at Bruche, Warrington for a three-month initial training course. It was a residential course and the accommodation was single rooms in large huts with communal toilets, washing and bathing facilities.

There were policewomen on the course but they had their own separate accommodation.

I was in 'B' syndicate and lads from the same intake and other syndicates shared our accommodation. Mike King was always singing the popular song 'Diana'. He left the police service to become a successful professional comedian. There was a great camaraderie and it was always good to meet some of my 'B' syndicate in the years to come. Inevitably, you lose contact with colleagues from other areas. Frank Moran was in the same accommodation block but I did not meet him after Bruche, until I took charge of Traffic and Uniform Operations some 28 years later, when I learned he was one of my Motorway constables.

Blackpool Borough used to issue second-hand uniforms and it was not always the best fit. I was sent to Bruche with a hat that was clearly too small. I had commented on this when it was issued to no avail. However, when I was at Bruche I was told to get a hat which was the correct size. Someone must have contacted Blackpool because I had no difficulty then in changing it.

Our class leader was Sergeant Archibald, a kindly man. Mick Reedy was the drill sergeant who I think struggled with me bearing in mind I did not do National Service. Sergeant Barnes was the swimming instructor. He was a good instructor and he told us that when we were in the pool, he was not shouting at us personally but getting his message through to our brain. Well, he succeeded with me. From an absolute non-swimmer, he taught me to swim and even achieve my Bronze Lifesaving Medallion. He later said that he got more pleasure and satisfaction from the achievements of students who previously could not swim, than from the higher awards earned by accomplished swimmers.

We had to study the law, mainly using Moriarty's Police Law, learn definitions, undertake first aid training and of course drill and physical training. I was ill for a few days at one time during my Bruche stay and I had to see the medic and these basic single rooms in the large huts were not good places to recuperate.

At that time I was the youngest Bobby in the Blackpool Force. Amusingly, the first motorist I reported for summons turned out to be the father of Rick Armstrong. Rick is my niece Julie's husband, although I did not know Mr Armstrong. When reported, he replied that I was too young to be a Bobby! Life is full of coincidences – as a butcher boy, I used to deliver meat to Mrs Armstrong.

Tony Cross' sister married Martin Wilson. Martin was the brother of Lyndon, the bright lad who passed his National Meat Diploma examination first time. At one time, Lyndon did own a butcher's shop in Marton. The Wilsons were very much a Marton family. Martin's brother Sam Wilson was a handyman and did some work for us when we lived in Kipling Drive. Martin however became a policeman. He was a first class Detective Sergeant.

In his retirement, Martin was a director/trustee and chairman of Disability Services (Blackpool, Wyre and Fylde) Ltd., a registered charitable company limited by guarantee. They provided the Rideabilty Bus Service, a service which offers disabled and housebound residents door-to-door transport. Martin regularly drove the bus and often picked up my late brother Jim, to take him to a community centre.

In 2017, the Rideabilty Service was taken over by Blackpool Council. When they handed over the service, Martin and fellow trustees had a surplus of £2,000. He gave me a cheque for that amount for the Superintendent Gerald Richardson Memorial Youth Trust. Martin's son Lee, also a policeman is the Chief Inspector in charge of the Blackpool area. Lee is also a valued trustee of the Gerry Richardson Trust. You will read more of the Trust later.

CHAPTER SIX
ON THE BEAT

Foot patrol life consisted of three shifts, 6am to 2pm (earlies), 2pm to 10pm (lates) and 10pm to 6am (nights). It sometimes worked out that you finished nights at 6am and had to be back on duty that day at 2pm. You had to get in to the police station 30 minutes prior to your starting time. You had to write in your pocket book details of any crimes or wanted persons. National Express Messages e.g. murder suspects were printed out but you had to put these into your book. If you had to hand write down all the murders nationally today, you would never be able to leave the office. Technology has certainly helped in some areas.

We paraded for duty 15 minutes prior to the start time e.g. 1.45pm for the late shift. If you were late you were charged from the parade time not your start time. This happened to me on one occasion when I got in at 6.30am. I was charged with being 45 minutes late. I even had to appear before Mr Harry Barnes, the Chief Constable, for a reprimand.

The parades were formal in full uniform. That was no problem as you had to report for duty in full uniform. The sergeant or inspector would bring the parade to attention; the command 'Produce appointments' would be given. You then had to produce your staff (truncheon) and handcuffs. If you did not have them with you, you were in trouble. I was proud of my handcuffs which were the old screw type because I had paid good money to have them chromed!

Blackpool Borough Police would probably have won any 'Thrift' award. When my trousers started to wear thin, I could not get them replaced and Kathleen had to darn them! We had choker collar tunics for winter and for night duty. My poor neck got chaffed but some of the old sweats liked the tunics, because they could wear their collarless shirts a few times and save washing! In the daytime in summer we wore open neck tunics but had to attach the collars and wear a black police tie. I hated fastening the collars to the shirt with the collar studs.

I was lucky because there were some police houses close to our home in Penrose Avenue. Consequently, PC Bill Rimmer, *a Dixon of Dock Green* type of Bobby, took me under his wing. We would cycle into work together and he was a great help. If I was on a beat which covered Penrose Avenue, my mother used to leave a flask of coffee out in the back yard for me and any other Bobby with me e.g. mentor.

Mum cherished all her sons. I once came across my younger brother Patrick and some of his friends when I was on night duty. They were being rowdy. I had words with them and brother Patrick started to show off in front of his mates and was very lippy. I wasn't having that and I said, "Behave yourself Meadows or you'll be the first to get locked up".

That quietened them down. I worked the full night shift and went to bed as soon as I got home. However, when I woke up my mother gave me a scolding for upsetting Patrick and told me not to get big headed!

Kathleen and I were married on 4 October 1958 at Elim Pentecostal Church. All the guys from my shift decided I should be taken for a drink on the night before I got married. At that time, I was a non-drinking, non-swearing and good living lad. We went across to the South Shore Hotel and I had my first taste of beer. My colleagues were concerned trying to ensure that I was OK. Two or three of them decided I should be escorted home. I am sure it was a comical sight three or four coppers in full uniform pedalling home on bikes. I thought I'll show these guys and I started to cycle fast and the older chaps were really pushed to keep up with me.

I was in good order on my wedding day and we had a nice wedding ceremony, my brother John was my best man. Kathy's wedding dress had been made by a friend and she looked absolutely stunning and she had four bridesmaids. We had the reception at the New Central Hotel in Blackpool. It was a memorable day.

Of course when we got married, having had to obtain written permission from the Chief Constable, we moved into rented accommodation. We rented the upstairs of a house in Worsley Avenue, South Shore. The old lady who owned it was very security conscious, to the degree that if ever there was a bad house fire we could never have got out in time. She used to double lock the front and vestibule door and lodge a piece of wood between the two to make it burglar proof. Kathleen did not like sleeping on her own, so when I was on night duty her sister used to sleep with her. However, when I got home Rose had to get up so I could get into bed to get my sleep. Talk about hot bedding!

After being on duty on a snowy night Kathleen woke me up after I had been asleep for a couple of hours to tell me that it had been snowing during the night!

At one time Kathleen and Rose fell out and Rose would not stop with her at night-time. Kathleen did not like sleeping in the dark so she left the light on, only to be told by Mrs Heptonstall that she had forgotten to switch the light off! It did not help when Mrs Heptonstall showed Kathleen her shroud ready for her burial.

We did not stay in Worsley Avenue for long and moved to the top floor police flat at 64 Dean Street. It was very handy for walking to work. The flat below was occupied by PC Frank Doyle and his wife Jeannie and their two daughters Yvonne and Kathy. We were happy there and we became good friends. One night Kathleen was looking after the girls because Frank was on duty, as I was, and Jeannie was working at the Cocktail Bar in the White Tower at Blackpool Pleasure Beach. Kathleen was awoken by a policeman shining a light in her face. He told her to get up and asked where her parents were. He asked her who she was and she replied indignantly, "I am Mrs Meadows". He did not realise that she was a married woman.

Ours was a huge flat and could not be fully furnished, we had another floor above us which was left unfurnished. The bath had a brown stain, I said earlier that Blackpool Borough was thrifty, no new bath for us, they kept sending a chap to paint it. After a short while the paint bubbled and you could peel it off, that went on for some time. Nevertheless, we were happy there and our next move was a police house on Troutbeck Crescent, Mereside, opposite the windmill and close to the main A583 road into Blackpool.

Any young police officer would be in company with an experienced officer for a period of time. One of the officers I went out with was Arthur Buckley and on one beat we called into a bowling club. We were warmly greeted by the steward who pulled Arthur a pint. I did not drink so I had a soft drink and a pork pie. We chatted away and then the steward got a note book out and made a note of what we had. Arthur enquired what he was doing.

"Don't worry Arthur. To keep the books right I just make a note of what you have had and the date, the committee are OK with that as long as I keep a record. Don't worry I don't put any names down".

Arthur said, "You don't need to, the date would identify us"! He never called in again on duty.

I was being shown round on one occasion by another Bobby, Frank, he was a lovely chap with a bit of a lisp. At Foxhall Square he saw a courting couple in a parked car, the car was not displaying lights. Frank went over and told the driver to switch his lights on. Sometime later we saw the car and the driver was attempting to start the engine but his car battery was flat. This amused Frank and he really had a good laugh and not being chivalrous, we did not offer to push the car.

Frank was once giving evidence at Quarter Sessions when the management of the Royal Pavilion Theatre were being prosecuted, apparently, one of the nude models had moved or something similar. Frank had been on plain clothes duty inside keeping observations. Representing the theatre was barrister George Carman, who later became one of the top Queen's Counsel (QC). He was trying to get some favourable reply, which was a well-used tactic of defence lawyers.

Carman said to Frank, "Come officer, you are a man of the world," to which Frank replied, "No sir, I've never been out of Great Britain". There were no more questions.

When on one occasion, I was not being at all favourable to a defendant, and the well-respected solicitor John Budd said, "Come come Mr Meadows, don't be uncharitable". He was always civil and dignified. John Budd later became HM Coroner for the Blackpool and the Fylde in 1968 and serve with distinction for some 20 years. Under the nom-de-plume of Julian Prescott, John Budd wrote eleven crime novels.

We were given practical assistance on how to do the job, for example, there was a stop sign at the bottom of South Park Drive, Blackpool for vehicles entering Preston New Road (A583). We were instructed to stand behind a big tree, from where you had sight of the junction. However, the drivers could not see you and you caught quite a few motorists failing to stop at the halt sign at the junction.

That junction featured in one incident shortly after I was released on the public unaccompanied. There was a report of a road traffic accident at that junction and I attended the scene. A man was injured and a private ambulance stopped and the driver offered to take him and me to hospital, inexperienced as I was, I accepted. Later at hospital, traffic officers attended and told me in no uncertain terms I should not have used the private ambulance and I should never have left the scene unattended. Of course we had no personal radios in those days and the nearest police pillar was at Oxford Square quite some distance away.

I later had to attend a fatal road traffic accident at the junction of Preston New Road and Preston Old Road. If my memory serves me right, work was being carried out to construct a dual carriageway. A young man was taken to Victoria Hospital and I attended with my sergeant, what I remember clearly was seeing the lad's parents leaving the hospital after being told their beloved son had died; they seemed to age before my eyes. The car driver involved was the first person in Blackpool to be charged with causing death by dangerous driving under the new 1960 Road Traffic Act.

My life as a beat Bobby was full of interesting moments, some good, some not so good. For example, it was not pleasant being detailed to stand in a back alley following reports of a prowler. I was ordered to remain there for four hours and it rained heavily all that time!

We worked a fixed beat system which meant we had to religiously follow the routes set out in our beat book, although sometimes they reversed the order of working. Today, people yearn for the Bobby on the beat, I accept that it gives confidence to see a Bobby. However, I remember a resident saying to me, "You know we can set our clocks from the time you pass here". I thought so can the burglars!

If you had to work seven beat reverse, you were supposed to walk from the police station (near to the South Pier, Blackpool) to Knowsley Avenue/West Park Drive (adjacent to Stanley Park) in 30 minutes, a distance of about three kilometres. Some sergeants would allow you to jump on a tram to Oxford Square, but not Trapper and we'll hear more of him later.

One day I was working number seven beat which was a two hour beat. I had walked out of Arnott Road at Spen Corner and started to walk along Hawes Side Lane towards the Police Station (now demolished, but it was opposite Crossland Road). As I was passing the Lane Ends Pub a Hillman car pulled up, I was being visited by the Deputy Chief Constable, Walter Warren.

"What are you doing here"?

I thought that perhaps I should have been working reverse order. I said words to the effect, "Sorry Sir, am I on the wrong half hour"?

"No", was his retort. "You should have been at Spen Corner", which was only about 200 yards away. All upset he continued, "I was going to give you 4.20pm at Spen Corner, now I'll have to make it 4.22pm at the Lanes Ends".

Clearly, I was walking too fast.

You had to record these visits in your pocket book which was regularly checked. You also were responsible for 'ALL STREETS AND PROPERTY ABUTTING THERETO'. Whatever happened, they had you by the 'short and curlies'. This meant that you had to physically check every shop and factory door on night duty. If a report was received of a burglary or damage to a property on your beat, you were dug out of your bed and had to report to the police station and submit a report. Well, so much for 'the good old days'. Moreover, if some resident went away on holiday they would ring up and their homes would be placed on an observation list. Regular checks had to be made on these properties, although you would find most of the side gates etc locked!

South Shore policing area included Marton. The southerly boundary was Squires Gate Lane and School Road (the boundary with St Annes) and its northerly boundary extended to Chapel Street (opposite Central Pier).

There were some really spooky places and there were two areas where you had to walk into an enclosed square to examine property. There was only one way in and out, it was old property and in some cases you had to go up outside staircases to check the upper floors. In the depth of winter when gales were blowing these locations became more eerie and one could hear all sorts of noises. I suspected that some officers took a chance and did not enter these squares in Dover Road and Cowley Road, I once heard some of the chaps talking about one colleague who walked down the middle of the road when he passed church graveyards and cemeteries.

The golden rule was that whatever happened; do not be late for your half hour point. The beats were separated into half hour sections. At the end of that half hour you had to wait for five minutes before setting off. That was likely to be the time you would get a visit from a sergeant or senior officer. One night, I came across a chap who was worth checking out, there were no personal radios or public phones nearby, so you had to satisfy yourself as to his bona fides as best you could. Carrying out this check meant that I was late for a point. The Inspector was waiting. He was a decent chap – a long serving detective before he was promoted uniform Inspector. He was very interested in what I had done but his parting words were, "Well done, but try not to be late for your point". In my naivety, I asked him what I should do in those circumstances and his reply was something like, "Do your best". On one cold frosty night I was at Hawes Side Police Station, a cold uninviting building, when a car turned up and there was the same Inspector and a sergeant. They brought in an urn of steaming hot coffee. This was unheard of but very welcome.

The lack of any means of communication meant that it was not uncommon if you arrested anyone; to take the prisoner to the police station by taxi. The taxi driver would then be reimbursed.

We had one particular sergeant nicknamed 'Trapper'. To ascertain if we had 'rattled the door handles' he would put unused matches on the latches of the handles, returning later to see if they were still in position. Arthur Buckley put a stop to that. He went and struck every match and replaced them!

Trapper loved animals but we felt that his love did not extend to policemen. On night duty, beats were often doubled up after 2am. I well remember one occasion, after 2am I was detailed for six and seven beats. The practice was to take a bicycle so you could cover the two beats. However, on this particular night it was snowing. I suggested that it might be more practical not to take the bike. "No" said Trapper – I had to take the bike which made it very difficult. In Back Cunliffe Road there was some factories and snow had drifted to a depth of two feet or more; I had to drag the bike along. I made my 4am point at Spen Corner feeling pretty miserable, when a taxi then came along and stopped. The rear passenger window was wound down to about three inches. I could see Trapper's beady eyes. He only spoke to give me visit i.e. "4 o'clock, Spen Corner" and as he wound his window up shouted, "This will test you"! He was not my favourite sergeant.

If we were needed, the light on the blue police pillars used to flash. These pillars were placed at various locations. If you made a point at one of these pillars you had to ring in. One night I was checking the Oxford Cinema. I checked a front door and to my horror, it opened. I thought how lucky I was because there was a police pillar 20 yards away. I crept up to the pillar, rang South Police Station and whispered, "I have found the Oxford Pictures open".

If you have ever watched *Heartbeat*, I would swear that the character Alf Ventress was modelled on our station duty man. I have to say, I received no comforting words, I was simply asked, "Have you checked it"?

I said, "What on my own"?

All I got then was "This is the trouble; you can't put an old head on young shoulders". No real advice was given.

Now I thought the station duty man would have got the traffic car and some assistance to cover the back to prevent any escape if burglars were inside. Not a cat in hell's chance of that happening, so I bit the bullet and went inside. It was pitch black and I only had my torch to guide me through the building. There was no break-in, no problem although there could have been. When I was checking behind the giant screen I tripped and nearly fell through the screen. It transpired the key holder, the projectionist who was courting the daughter of our next door neighbour, had not secured the cinema door.

An old sergeant Peter McNab once said to me, "By the time you reach 21 laddie, you'll be a man". Peter McNabb was a real character, one day I was on point duty on the Promenade outside the Casino, Pleasure Beach. Peter was stood next to me. I was facing north and gave the stop signal to traffic travelling south. A Bedford Dormobile vehicle was the first vehicle which should have stopped. It was full of black people. The driver just ignored my stop signal and carried on whereupon Peter jumped on his bike, and with the traffic being slow he caught up with the vehicle at Watson Road. He had his day stick and brought it down on the van with a resounding thud. The driver was petrified and after a stern reprimand was allowed to go. I think in the future, he would stop for any police signal.

Peter also came to my rescue once, I was outside the Wellington and Pier Hotel on Central Promenade and I was arresting two men when they started to fight with me. I was not going to let them go and I struggled. No one came to my assistance. However, a tram driver travelling south along the promenade was stopped at the Central Pier. He had to carry on driving his tram, but when he got to the Queens Hotel, South Promenade, he stopped the tram and ran into South Shore Police Station in Montague Street where he saw Peter told him what he had seen. Peter got into his own car, picked up another Bobby en route and I was still struggling with the two men when Peter arrived and they were duly locked up.

There were some real characters. My brother John, his wife Agnes and her sister Jane lived at Newhouse Farm on the corner of Preston New Road and Cherry Tree Road North. We often visited and on one summer evening heard a noise in the orchard, the chickens were squawking. We ran into the orchard and someone had obviously jumped over the fence. The only person in view was a local *Heartbeat* 'Greengrass' character who lived on Marton Moss. I told him I was a policeman. He denied being in the orchard. I could not prove it but he was clearly after some chickens!

On one cold winter's night I was patrolling the Marton Moss area and was at the point at the junction with School Road and Midgeland Road, near the boundary with St Annes. It was foggy and icy and I had on my overcoat and a cape, you could not run fast in this gear! I looked at my cape and I was covered in what appeared to be wisps of cotton wool. It was the mist freezing, just like candy floss.

On night duty during the summer season and illuminations we were detailed for duty at the Pleasure Beach Coach Park. Trouble could be expected at closing time particularly from some elements that travelled from Liverpool on the Crown and Home James Coaches. You hoped you would be with a good mate who would stay the course, some of the more timid or lazy ones would arrest someone for a minor drunk charge and that would take them into the police station until their prisoner had been booked in and charged; some officers never reappeared.

On one occasion, my colleague Tony Cross and I were detailed to escort the pop star Cliff Richard into the South Pier when he arrived. Chief Inspector Butterworth said he should be protected from being crowded but reminded us that these celebrities wanted to greet their fans. When Cliff arrived it was very crowded and there could have been a problem escorting him in. Tony was as tall as me so we each grabbed an arm and whisked him onto the pier. I don't think his feet touched the ground and he winced when I grabbed his arm!

With John Smalley, I had to look after a film crew who were filming an advert for Super National Benzole petrol. The actors posed in a white open topped saloon and drove along the tram track. The photographer took a nice picture of us and there was only one mishap, the cameraman had to lie horizontally across the back of the vehicle. He was so engrossed in his filming that he failed to see a tram stop and hit his head with a sickening thud and I think he went to hospital. The finished advert was quite popular and the jingle was *'It's a joy ride with Super National Benzole'*.

My first publicity in *The Gazette* was printed under the headline, 'PC SAVED TRAPPED BUDGIE IN FIRE'. I came across a house fire in St Annes Road, the householders Mr and Mrs Clarke had evacuated the house, I called for the Fire Brigade and then I was told that their budgie was trapped in the fire. Mr Clarke had crawled back into the house but had only been able to unplug the radio set because of dense smoke. The lady was so distressed about her budgie so I went back in, visibility was very poor because of the smoke but I did retrieve Billy the budgie. What I did not tell Mrs Clarke was that the bird was on the floor and I nearly stood on it!

There are some matters which the complainant regards as serious but can still bring a smile to one's face. Crossland Road Park had a park attendant who was lame and limped and the local kids used to tease him. They would hide in the bushes opposite his office (which was an old air raid shelter) and shout "Hoppity, Hoppity". He would come to the door with his whip which was a cane with a piece of rope attached. Sometimes he chased them off but on other occasions he could not see where they were hiding. One day the kids shouted to him and he appeared at the office door whip in hand. He was about a yard outside and whilst trying to see where they were hiding, a young lad aged about seven or eight had climbed onto the concrete roof and then urinated on him. When he told me, I know I should not have done, but I could not help but smile.

After two years I had to appear before the new Chief Constable Harry Sanders. The purpose was to see if my probationary period had been successful when my appointment as a police constable would be confirmed. Not all probationary constables were kept on. The Chief Constable said he was happy with my progress and if I worked as I had done, he would be happy. He went on about how I could improve and suggested I take elocution lessons (I am a proud Lancastrian – I think he came from Bedford). He then went into areas which completely lost me, I asked him if he would explain what I needed to do. He said that I should go with Chief Inspector Stevenson, the Training Officer (who was present throughout) who would explain all. We went to Mr Stevenson's office. I sat down and he looked at me.

"Jeffrey," he said, "like you, I hadn't a clue what he was on about, so carry on doing what you are doing and you'll be fine".

One day I was driving home in my car (first car cost £27 10s). I turned from Lytham Road into Waterloo Road. There was a tram in the centre of the road with passengers boarding. It was dusk I gave the passengers a wide berth and as I passed I heard a bump. I stopped and a lady at the rear of the queue had small dog on the end of a very long lead. Of course the dog was not easy to spot, it was injured but did not seem serious and I took the lady to a veterinary surgeon. She thanked me but suggested I should pay the bill. I politely declined informing her that she had carelessly let her dog wander too far. It was evident that she was not paying attention.

I was given the job of timing a new six beat which was being evaluated. I went round the beat, it was a two hour beat but taking into account that on night duty you had to check property, there was no way in my view, that two hours was long enough. I reported back to the Chief Inspector and an Inspector. My evaluation was not greeted with enthusiasm, it was suggested that I had allowed too much time. I reminded them about checking property at night and if the time allowed was insufficient some burglaries or damage could be missed. The Chief Inspector said it was understandable that something may be missed. I knew that view would not be understood if there was a break-in which was not discovered. The Inspector said that that my timing was ridiculous and he would walk and time the beat himself. I must admit that it was with some satisfaction that I heard reports that he had got lost carrying out that task!

The Inspector was an ex guardsman, a man who was quite black and white in his views. One night I was patrolling four beat when I saw a troublemaker with a group of young lads. He was my age and had been troublesome at school and had been involved with a gang that caused a lot of damage at the New Ritz Cinema on Central Prom. He started catcalling, making fun of me and showing off to the younger lads. I had a quiet word with him and suggested if he wanted to have a go at me, I would be on that beat all night and he could see me later when he had got rid of his cronies and we could sort out any problems.

The next night when parading for duty, the Inspector said that he was very disappointed that one of his officers had threatened a young lad who was trying to go straight and get his life back on track, or words to that effect. The youth had gone in that evening to report me; a real tough guy! That was not the only reprimand I got from that Inspector, we used to park our cars without lights outside our row of police houses on Troutbeck Crescent, Mereside. A scooter PC reported three or four of us, he did not speak to us first, simply reported us to the Inspector. Of course a reprimand followed.

But this Inspector however, did complement me and a colleague on one occasion. CID had been keeping observations at a flat in South Shore for an escaped violent prisoner. Uniform officers were then requested to take over the observations, Roger Downing and I concluded that CID must have thought the prisoner would not turn up at the flat. Much to our surprise, the escaped prisoner turned up with three friends. We arrested them, CID officers were called and quickly took the wanted man to the police station, intending for other officers to take the three friends in. In the meantime, the Inspector arrived. He was very pleased that uniform officers had arrested the wanted man. He told us to 'take their names and addresses' of the three men before they left, I told him they were going nowhere because they were being arrested.

"Right", he said.

I was once on point duty on the Promenade at Manchester Square. Sgt Eric Collinge came to visit me. It was a busy point with tramcars crossing to the Promenade from Lytham Road and you had to keep your wits about you. Hearing a bang we looked onto the Promenade and we saw the legs of two ladies disappearing under a Double Decker balloon tram. They had been knocked down, but their lives were saved by the cow catcher at the front of the tram aided by the flat surface of the track. In some sections of the Promenade tram track, the lines were laid on sleepers similar to railway lines and had the accident happened at those sections, the outcome would not have been good. We later saw the ladies in hospital, they were badly bruised but made a recovery.

On 12 February 1959 I had to go by train to Exeter to escort a man wanted on a warrant. I was briefed by the then Detective Sergeant Alf Southern and was on my way. Alf wrote out clear instructions for me, I stayed overnight at the Ship Inn, Exeter for the price of 14 shillings and six pence. In those days it was not uncommon to send a single officer for a prisoner.

The prisoner turned out to be a member of the Royal Air Force and was in full uniform. On the long journey back I needed to pay a call. I handcuffed the prisoner to one of the heavy metal ashtrays. When I returned, I saw the prisoner standing in the corridor with his handcuff still attached to the ashtray.

On seeing me, he shouted, "Don't worry, I wasn't trying to escape. I'm joking".

We had to change trains at Crewe and went into the cafe. We were having brew when several Scottish soldiers in uniform came in. They saw that the RAF man was handcuffed and came up to us. They asked him if he wanted releasing. My prisoner was a Scot and told them he wanted to go back and sort his problem out.

"You're sure, they said".

He replied "Yes," and I was much relieved.

The practice of single officer escorts continued for some while. It only stopped when one of Jack Tebay's prisoners dived through a train window and local police forces had to search for the escaped prisoner.

There was a local villain called Larry Rushton, nicknamed Lasham. During the gun amnesty in the 1960's, I was at South Shore Police Station when he handed in several handguns with ammunition. I had seen Rushton in a vehicle one night and noted the time and car number in my pocket book. At a crime conference the senior detective asked for all officers to submit any information about Rushton. I told them I had seen him and noted it. This turned out to be critical evidence meaning he could be charged when he was released from Pentonville Prison. I was asked to go and arrest him on his release. Dougie Watson came with me. Dougie was a very good copper but could be laid back. He suggested we did not handcuff Rushton as there were two of us. I did not agree to this and told Dougie to put his coat over their lower arms to cover the handcuffs. We got him back safely. Rushton later acquired a considerable reputation as an artist and sold many of his paintings.

Betting shops did not become legal until 1 May 1961. We went with Kathleen's cousin Victor and his wife Valerie to visit her grandparents in Workington, we were royally looked after. Grandma was a great cook and we were fed well, even having a cooked supper. It was a nice break and we visited a few places in the North Lakes. On the Sunday we all met for Grandma's Sunday lunch, the lunch was excellent but there was constant knocking on the front door. Grandfather Tommy would go to answer the door and when he returned he was certainly uneasy. I spoke to Victor, who whispered that Tommy was a bookies' runner. I was a guest in their house and they kept sending punters away because they did not want to embarrass me, or wondered whether I would report them. I spoke to Tommy and told him that I was off duty and moreover, I was in Blackpool Borough Police, not the force which covered Workington.

With some sense of relief, he reached under the dining table and brought out a purpose made bookies' clock to time the bets. He was quite a busy bookies' runner. They were a lovely couple and the practice of illegal betting was common. In fact, Kathleen's granddad Thomas had been carted off once in a black Mariah for illegal betting!

I received my first commendation from the Chief Constable for recovering a stolen van. I was on night duty on a December evening and was checking the Daggers Hall Lane Social Club. I went into the back alley that also led up to the back of the Empire Cinema when I saw a van, I checked the vehicle over and shone my torch on the excise licence. The registered number on the licence was different to the registration plates on the vehicle. I reported this and an early duty officer kept surveillance. A local man returned to the vehicle and was arrested. Apparently he had stolen the van from a garage in Vicarage Lane between 1 and 2 December. The vehicle valued at £235 had been left for repair and the thief was fined £25 and was told by the Chairman Councillor T.B. Fairclough, "You have narrowly escaped going to gaol this morning. The magistrates have taken a lenient view because of your previous good character".

One of my last duties in uniform before being transferred to CID duties was keeping observations in Station Road toilets for men committing acts of gross indecency. Kathleen was in

Victoria Hospital about to give birth to Darren. Together with the then Sergeant Eddie Gray our instructions were to try and catch a persistent offender, a greengrocer. We were in a small broom cupboard, Eddie watched through the keyhole and I had to stand up and look through a tiny hole we had drilled through. We saw many distasteful acts but had been instructed to stay in hiding until the main target was committing an offence. The men always performed these acts in the public area, not the cubicles.

We were observing one day when two men came downstairs to the toilet. One man was a labourer type, whilst the other man was very smart and well-dressed. Without speaking the labourer type got down on his knees and committed an act of fellatio on the well-dressed man. The social order and status was certainly maintained! That was too much for us and we burst out, The well-dressed man exclaimed, "Good God", whilst for obvious reasons, the man on his knees could not speak. At committal proceedings I had to give oral evidence and the lady chairman listened very intently.

Because I could not visit the Maternity Ward at normal visiting hours, I got permission to visit outside visiting hours. Darren was born on 4 October 1962, our fourth wedding anniversary. He was a real blessing because our first child, a daughter was stillborn in St Anne's Hospital. It was a very traumatic time and whilst Kathy was recovering in hospital, I had to tell our family and friends and that certainly got to me.

I had been very keen on crime and had built up a reasonable reputation and was earmarked for CID duties. The system was that the Detective Sergeants, who could closely observe those who had some good crime arrests would have a meeting and recommend to the Detective Superintendent, which constables, should be transferred to CID. Transfers were announced on police orders, and after the publication of one police order, two of the Detective Sergeants came up to me and congratulated me. Having seen the orders, I had to tell them that my name was not on the list. They just could not believe it, I do not know how true it is, but I was told that Chief Constable Harry Sanders had blocked my name.

Shortly after that incident, a sergeant came to me, he told me that Sanders was transferring to Lancashire County as Assistant Chief Constable (Crime). The sergeant said that I should not complain about missing out in the last round of transfers to CID. The incoming Chief Constable Stan Parr had promised that I would be his first transfer to CID. He kept that promise very soon afterwards. I had been a beat Bobby for five years.

When I went on my Home Office Detective Training Course, Mr Sanders came to address the course members. When he saw me he asked, "When did you go into CID Meadows"? With some satisfaction I responded, "As soon as you left Sir"!

Stan Parr, the former Chief Constable of Lancashire certainly had his problems but I always found him to be a decent man. At Stan's funeral Canon Davies is reported as saying, "I, and I know a large body of people, believe that it was basically because of his kindness that he found himself in difficulties". I attended his funeral at St Stephens on the Cliff Church, Blackpool. The church was full.

Stan was a former well-respected member of Blackpool South Rotary Club. In his memory the club decided to award a silver salver to a member who made an outstanding contribution to the club and Rotary. The award which is made annually is in the gift of the President during their presidential year and is made at the annual Charter Dinner. I was privileged to win the Salver twice.

Ian Parr, one of Stan's three sons and a former member of South Ribble Rotary Club usually presents the award. Ian and his wife Catherine are friends and their son Chris and daughter Lauren are serving police officers. Chris a was Constable in Greater Manchester Police but approximately twelve months ago, transferred to Lancashire Constabulary being based at Headquarters in a Special Uniform Ops team. Laura is a Detective Sergeant in Merseyside. Their grandfather would be very proud of them.

CHAPTER SEVEN
JEFF BECOMES A JACK

Detectives were often referred to as Jacks, a slang word, there does not appear to be any definitive answer as to why the word Jacks is used. There is an interesting dialogue on the Australian website, 'The Word Detective'. The word 'Jack' is defined in the *Oxford Dictionary* as a Detective or Police Officer.

It was a dream come true to become a Jack. Although not a promotion, it was surprising how many members of the public saw it as such. I was transferred to Central CID working out of a converted house which was situated between the northerly end of the Main Police Station and the Fire Station on Albert Road.

My first sergeant was John Parkinson and I joined Detective Constables Ronnie Wilkinson and Don Cooper. I enjoyed working with them; they were older than me and had more experience so I could learn from them and you do learn lessons if you open your mind. I remember watching another experienced detective giving evidence, he told the magistrates that he cautioned the accused and when asked what the caution was, much to his dismay he got it wrong. Complacency can be your downfall.

We had been issued with cards with the various cautions on. Thereafter, whenever I cautioned anyone, I got the card out and read it to them. When giving evidence I told the Court that I read the caution to the accused/defendant from the card. I was often asked at Quarter Sessions (later Crown Courts) by the judge if I had that card with me, which I always had. I was then invited to read the caution from that card.

Blackpool Borough had 30 plus detectives, which was quite high for a borough force. We did split shifts, e.g. Day shift was 9am to 1pm and 2pm to 6pm. Late shift was 9am to 1pm and 6pm to 10pm. There was also an 8am to 4pm shift. There was a 6pm to 2am evening car with two detectives and a 10pm to 6am shift with two detectives. When on the day shift you were expected to come back on some evenings and when on late shift you were expected to come back some afternoons.

For several years there was no payment for overtime as a detective. When a national Home Office survey was carried out, at Blackpool South CID, the average quarterly unpaid overtime for a detective was 200 plus hours. Detectives later received a 'Supplementary Detective Allowance', this was worked out on the collective average hours overtime worked by the Federated Ranks.

One of the duties on the 8am to 4pm shift was to attend burglaries reported after 8am and we also had to visit the common lodging house in Seed Street to check arrivals etc. That was quite an experience and I remember on my first visit walking across the yard. A voice shouted out, "Hello Boss" or words to that effect. I looked and there was this vagrant type sat on the outside toilet, legs astride and totally unconcerned about who could see him. The actual 'lodgings' was a room with a load of men sleeping there and reminded me of a Dickensian scene.

My ramblings are not in any particular order, but it is nice to recall some of the experiences in CID, some good and some bad.

As I write this, the Oxford Cinema has long gone and next door was Thomas Motors Ltd, whose boss was Harry Dennison. The Thomas Motors building has been demolished recently to make way for a newly constructed Aldi Store on the corner of Waterloo Road and Park Road. On 12 May 2015, *The Gazette* reported that, "Planning permission for the Aldi includes a condition that the ground floor facade of the former Thomas Motors building is retained". The Aldi store is now open and is a modern store with a good size car park. At least some part of Thomas Motors remains, but another casualty of this building project was the demolition of the old Oxford Hotel.

I remember being called to Thomas Motors. I saw the owner Mr Dennison, he said he did not mind the lads in the paint shop doing any jobs on their own vehicles, however, the full team, perhaps of six or seven had started their own business using Thomas Motors workshops and material. In effect they were in direct competition with their own employer! They were all arrested, sacked and dealt with at Court.

At this time I worked at South CID. The jobs would come in overnight and one of the detective sergeants would allocate them. The job sheets were usually on the sergeant's desk and before they were allocated, we would have a quick look to identify the interesting ones. One such report was from Geoff Abbott who was the beat officer for the area covering Thomas Motors. His report was about an attempt to persuade an employee who worked on the night shift to fiddle the pumps. What was interesting about this case is that it was still not allocated to any detective, I spoke to the sergeant who said that this was a case of incitement to commit crime, commenting that the force had never had such a case in living memory. This sounded a really cracking case so I asked if I could take it, the sergeant agreed if I thought I could handle it and said I had to liaise with him if there were any problems. I got hold of a copy of *'Archbold Criminal Pleading, Evidence and Practice'*. This was the book lawyers and judges referred to.

Geoff Abbott had been a former detective and Drug Squad officer who had returned to uniform duties, he was sound officer. We interviewed the informant and obtained his statement. We had to get corroboration of the incitement, so we asked the informant to arrange a meet with the suspect, we had to brief the informant at some length to ensure that in any conversation he did not act as an agent provocateur. Geoff and I were in an upstairs room and we could see them and hear any dialogue between the two. The suspect arrived and went into some details how they could fiddle the petrol invoices, we got sufficient evidence to apply for a warrant which was granted. One morning Geoff and I went to the offender's factory. He was sat in his office with his feet on the desk.

"Hello lads are you OK?" he asked.

I said, "We are but you won't be in a minute". I read out the warrant of arrest. He was quite shocked and he was later dealt with successfully at court.

Juveniles, or 'ankle biters' as we nicknamed them, could be quite difficult to deal with. They looked like 'butter wouldn't melt in their mouths'. They would look you in the face and then often tell you a pack of barefaced lies.

We were called to a fancy goods shop in South Shore where the owners had detained about five juveniles. They went down in size from the eldest who was about 13 years old to about six or seven years old, they reminded me of the children from the film *'The Sound of Music'*. Apparently, they had walked into the shop in single file and without stopping had stolen goods from the counters, an Aunt who was in charge of them was arrested and appeared at Court the next morning for remand. Two females from Liverpool appeared and wanted to stand bail for her, I recall that they said they had brought the defendant's 'rent book'. Whilst they were in court, we nipped out and checked their vehicle. The boot was empty but had been lined with paper. We suspected that once their friend was freed from Court, they would be going on a 'shoplifting expedition'. We did have words with them and advised them to return to Liverpool as soon as the remand had been dealt with. We later learned that the children were taken onto the Kop at Liverpool Football Club and trained to 'dip', i.e. stealing people's wallets etc.

We arrested one individual for offences which included stealing ladies knickers. He received a custodial sentence for an offence he had committed in Yorkshire, he was produced to appear at Bradford Quarter Sessions and I was called to give evidence. I got there late afternoon and in accordance with common practice, I was taken out in the evening by West Yorkshire detectives. We paid a visit to a Bradford Casino and we had a flutter on the dice table, as the guest, I was invited to throw the dice. The croupier was a very attractive young lady and I was captivated by her décolletage and I threw the dice and completely missed the table!

At Court, the next morning the accused appeared. The clerk asked him his home address emphasising the word home.

The reply was, "Armey Jail".

He was asked a couple more times for his home address without success. One of the victims was an attractive lady, and the prosecutor said to the prisoner that he must have noticed that an attractive lady lived at the house, from where he had stolen the knickers. His reply was that he did not know who lived there or words to that effect.

Trying to emphasise the point the prosecutor said, "Come, Come, Miss Meadows is a good looking young woman".

There was much hilarity as he had confused my name with the young lady's name. After the trial, the accused was sent back to his 'home', Armley Jail!

If detectives came to Blackpool, they would be looked after. We often received CID officers from London. One night two Metropolitan detectives arrived to take back a prisoner arrested in Blackpool. My colleague and I took them out and introduced them to top British Boxer Ronnie Clayton who was licensee of The Lion Hotel on South Promenade. We later received a report from the Met informing us of the result of the case when the accused had appeared at Court. The final paragraph thanked us for looking after the detectives so well whilst in Blackpool. That was a first, to receive thanks in that type of report. The main detective constable was called John Stevens, later to become the Commissioner of the Metropolitan Police and later elevated to the House of Lords.

If you talked to old detectives they would say that you got information from the pubs. I think that view is only partly true.

Detectives were encouraged to go into drinking establishments and were given expenses for any money spent on cultivating an informant or spending on them, 'grass' being the common term for an informant. For example you might buy them a drink or some cigarettes. The amount allowed was a modest amount and any money spent had to be recorded and was thoroughly checked by the supervising officers. I was of the view that information did not necessarily come from informants in pubs per se, it was important for any detective to visit a hostelry without causing a stir and that could only happen if you visited often, and not just when you wanted information.

There were some pubs where the clientele was so anti-police or frightened of police that as soon as you walked in, the pub went quiet and the chatter stopped till you walked out. The Talbot Inn, near Talbot Road Bus Station was one such pub. A drunken male hit a barmaid over the head with a bar stool, of course, no one wanted to talk to us but I managed to find out where the attacker lived. It was close to the pub where the assault had taken place. I was on my own when I got the information, so I went to make enquiries, it was in the afternoon and I went into the suspect's flat and much to my surprise the man responsible was asleep on a couch. I woke him up, had a chat and he agreed to come to the CID Office. I had no transport so I walked him to the CID office in Albert Road. However, when he got there he must have realised he was going to be locked up and he suddenly went berserk and it took several officers to restrain him. I guess I was lucky that day and the man was charged and successfully dealt with at Court.

That was not the first time I had walked a 'suspect' to the office, when I was at South CID Office a call came in to advise us that there had been an assault at the South Pier. I was told that the person thought to be responsible was none other than Dominic Pye, the well-known wrestler.

No other detective volunteered and according to my colleagues, it was my turn for a job! With a uniform Bobby I walked to the

Pier and took the long walk to the theatre at the end of the Pier where wrestling matches were taking place. The complainant said that Dominic Pye had assaulted him.

Now Dominic Pye was a man mountain character. He was huge and at one time turned a car over in Blackpool Town Centre when the driver annoyed him! I spoke to Dominic, he was aware of the complaint but said it was something and nothing or words to that effect. I said we needed to sort it out and he agreed to come to the CID Office. He was absolutely no trouble and made a statement. When I investigated further, it was clear that there was insufficient evidence to substantiate a charge.

Many years later on 26 February 1979, Dominic was killed in a shotgun accident at his property in Singleton, he was 50 years of age. The gun was found to have some sort of defect.

Word came from the Hospital Staff that a young lady had been taken in; she had given birth and the baby had lived for a brief time then died. It transpired that she had been the subject of a criminal abortion. The CID was now investigating a crime of criminal abortion and manslaughter. The young lady lived on the Marton Moss.

I was working at the South Shore CID Office at the time. Detective Inspector Bob Crompton was dealing with the case and he worked from Central CID Office. He telephoned and said we had to meet him that evening, when he arrived at South CID he said to me, "You are a local lad. Where are we going to find the answer to this one"?

I suggested that we may find the answer in one of four pubs, The Rag (the Lane Ends) on Hawes Side Lane, The Welcome and Railway Inn on Vicarage Lane (now the Hungry Horse), the Highfield Hotel or the Shovels both on Common Edge Road.

That evening, together with Detective Inspector Crompton and a colleague from South CID, we visited the Lane Ends but no useful information was gleaned. Our next stop was the Highfield Hotel. We ordered a drink and waited till an opportunity presented itself for me to have a quiet chat with a chap who I knew would have his 'ear to the ground'. He was not a usual informant but was a regular at the pub and knew me and other CID officers from South CID. I quietly told him what had happened. He showed no surprise and told me who he thought was responsible and where he lived. Apparently the suspect was a nightwatchman at a brick works just outside the borough boundary. The good news was that he lived in our area.

The next morning we gave him an early morning call and the Detective Inspector arrested him. The prisoner then decided he wanted to use the loo, he was allowed to but he had to keep the door open and I was on guard. He complained bitterly saying that what we were making him do gave him no dignity. I found that an astounding statement because our enquiries revealed that he had been carrying out abortions in a dirty shed at the brick works. He had made a copper tube specially to carry out the abortions. He was duly convicted and jailed for a long time.

We had another case of illegal abortions. Another Detective Inspector, John Brown was in charge of the case, he had a warrant to search a house in South Shore. I was part of the team and I was asked to cover the back and I climbed over the gate. As I approached the kitchen, I saw the suspect inside trying to escape in my direction. The back door was locked. Lifting my leg (which I could not do now!) and with one thud, I forced the door kicking at the lock. The door swung wide open and remarkably, there was no damage. I was never able to repeat that successful entry using my feet. The suspect was arrested and was due to appear the next morning for a further remand in custody.

I left early with the Detective Inspector Brown and we travelled to the Isle of Wight to interview an important witness, we needed evidence because the suspect had been charged with words to the effect, 'At a date and place unknown, did administer an unknown noxious substance to an unknown female with intent to cause an illegal abortion'. Detective Superintendent Sanders was to oppose bail. Fortunately as enquiries continued, sufficient evidence was gained to charge the man and he was successfully prosecuted.

I was on duty on the night CID car with Detective Sergeant Dave Heaney at about 3am on Saturday 29 March 1969. As we were travelling north along the Promenade, we caught sight of a house fire in a house in Bairstow Street. We turned round and as we approached the house fire it was quite eerie. It was a still night and the house fire was very advanced, flames leaping about twenty feet above the roof, yet there was no activity at all. We radioed the control room requesting the fire brigade. We ran into the house and saw the householder, a man we knew standing on the staircase. He was only wearing vest and underpants and his hair was on fire. On seeing us he said, "Thank God you're here lads. My baby's upstairs". Despite several attempts we could not get upstairs to rescue his two-year-old son. The fire raged out of control and burning timber was dropping, preventing us reaching the first floor. In his desperation, he thought we could save his child but we failed to do so and the baby perished. It was a most humbling experience that we were not able to live up to his expectations and save his baby son.

His 15-year-old nephew acted gallantly saving his young baby sister and three-year-old brother from upstairs and then made sure that his five sisters who had been sleeping downstairs were safely out of the building.

Even in those circumstances there was some humour, perverse though it may have been, the fire brigade arrived promptly so Dave and I started to evacuate nearby residents. We went next door and spoke to the occupier, an elderly man. We made sure he had a coat on and escorted him across the road to safety, he then said that he had to go back. We explained that the house next door was on fire and the fire could easily spread to his home. However, he ran back to his house and we had to stop him. We asked what was so important.

His reply was, "I have to back my fire up; I don't want my fire to go out"!

One night Dave and I caught a couple of lads breaking into a cigarette machine in Deansgate opposite the Blackpool Bus Station. On seeing us they ran off, we gave chase and arrested them. They were convicted but in their defence, they said they were running away because they thought two thugs were chasing them. I did sport very long sideburns at the time but I do not think we looked like two thugs, or did we? To this day Dave and I address one another as Thuggy!

One Friday I was with Dave and DC Chris Wood on the night CID car, Chris had joined us because his vehicle had broken down. A call came out that burglars had been disturbed in the Canada Crescent area which is the Bispham area of town. Other patrols had gone to the scene so we decided to cruise round the area, we had passed the Squirrel Pub travelling towards Bispham Village Centre when we saw two young men come out of the driveway of a house on Bispham Road, the rear of which would back onto the Canada Crescent property. We stopped and one look told us we had the offenders. Their jeans were covered in mud. We arrested them and radioed in.

We then got a message, "Can you keep them there".

Apparently, a new police dog was being trained and they wanted to see if it could follow the trail to the prisoners. From the driveway of a house about 50 yards away, this big black Alsatian appeared. Its paws looked the size of a small shovel. We got back into the CID car having told the prisoners not to run because the dog could run faster than them. As the dog got closer, the two men pressed themselves as close to the wall as they could. What happened next was hilarious. The dog walked past the two men, whereupon the dog man who was supervising, grabbed hold of the dog, turned it round to face the prisoners and slapped its rump saying, "Good dog"!

The two men were remanded in custody the next day. To encourage the new dog handler, in my one page report (which was all you had to submit for a remand in those days) I mentioned that the dogs had assisted the search.

The following night, I was preparing the prosecution file when the new dog handler came into the CID Office, I asked the nature of his visit. He replied that he had come to give a witness statement, I was curious and asked what evidence he thought he could give.

"The dog had identified the prisoners," he told me. I wondered whether I had been involved in the same incident. I asked how the dog had identified the men.

"It pointed towards them with his tail".

I think he actually believed it! I have to say, that 'evidence' did not appear in the file. Years later the same officer was a good solid detective.

One night I was in the Lifeboat Inn on Foxhall Road chatting to the landlord Arthur Nelson. Suddenly there was a loud crash and a man came flying into the pub. He had been outside when some yobs had picked him up and threw him through a plate glass window. I ran outside and started to chase them. I heard the sound of running feet behind me and when I looked, some locals from the pub, some of whom were local miscreants were following.

One shouted something like, "We're with you Jeff".

We caught some of the group and because they denied it an identification parade had to be arranged. The night Detective Sergeant said he would get some lads for the line-up. There is humour in the job and three Sikhs complete with beards and turbans turned up at the Charge Office saying they had volunteered to go with the line-up. The Detective Sergeant was having a joke, it had to be explained to them that we could not use them as the suspects were young white males, they were gracious and left. We did manage to get enough people for a parade which was no mean feat because they only got a shilling and many had come on coach trips and had a tight schedule. The parade was successful and the offenders were charged.

I was on the night CID car on one occasion, my partner had gone off early as he was to attend court the next morning. I was dealing with a report of a burglary at a social club in North Shore when I got a call to say that there was suspicious death in the Bairstow Street area. I attended the scene and went upstairs into a back bedroom. A uniform Inspector and Sergeant were present. As I walked in, the sergeant in a theatrical motion pulled the bedclothes back shouting 'Ta da' as if he was introducing some act. What confronted my eyes was a mummified body.

Entering into the spirit, I said:

> It reminds me of the young Indian brave.
> Who found a dead squaw in a cave.
> He said, "How disgusting.
> It only needs dusting.
> And look at the money I'll save".
> Boom, Boom.

The Inspector who was not known for his sense of humour retorted, "Typical CID" and they left.

The interesting thing was that there was no trace of any blow flies. This was because the door had been left closed and windows shut, although there may not have been a window. What I did find was many packets of cold fish and chips and there were several chamber pots under the bed which were full! I called the Detective Superintendent out. He started to search and put his hand in one of the chamber pots not realising they were full. You have to have these moments to lighten your day!

We went to the mortuary and the Home Office pathologist attended, he was quite excited at what he described as a perfect mummification. He asked me to go to the car and fetch his sample jars. I could only find large empty toffee jars which turned out to be the sample jars. After a considerable time, the pathologist stated that he had been able to identify every major organ but he could not give us a cause of death at that time. Further tests would have to be carried out at his base.

I went home and hung my overcoat on the line to give it a good blow as there is always a 'death' smell at post mortems. When Kathy saw it she asked why my coat was on the line. When I explained, I thought I would not be allowed in the bed again.

There was a lodger at the deceased's flat. He had come to Blackpool from his home in Wales and said that the deceased was a very nice lady who had been more of a mother to him than his own. Apparently she had been dead for 11 months and during that time he had brought her fish and chips and slept in the same bed! Enquiries revealed that there was no foul play, but he had committed offences in relation to concealing her body. In explaining his actions he said that he thought the world of this lovely lady and when he found her dead he could not bring himself to move her and tell anyone. Was his actions noble though misguided? You might have been drawn to that conclusion except we discovered that he had been drawing her pension for the 11 months and of course, he ended up in Court!

There was one elderly so-called blind man who was always hanging round parks and was a threat to young children. He had been brought in a few times but managed to get away with it saying he was just in the park and could hardly see any children. He was a nasty individual. One day I was in a CID car with a couple of colleagues returning from Divisional Headquarters when we saw him near a park. By chance we saw a magistrate nearby, so we asked him if he could spare time to keep the man under surveillance. He readily agreed. We saw this 'blind man' approaching young children so we went to arrest him. As I grabbed hold of him, he turned looked at me and said, "You black bastard", a reference to my black hair. So much for being blind!

The CID building in Albert Road was an old house. When you walked in the back way, there was an old slop stone sink (where I once skinned and dressed a hare for a Detective Sergeant). You then did a left turn and almost immediately turned right into the main corridor. However, if you turned right too soon you would walk into the cellar door. I had been out on patrol with Keith Witherington and we entered by the back door, Keith was striding ahead, it was all in darkness and then I heard a shout. Someone had left the cellar door open and Keith had fallen down the cellar steps.

I helped him up. He had broken his lower arm and the bone was protruding. He was muttering "Petty economy", a reference to the light being off. I decided to take him to hospital in my car. He sat in the front passenger seat and I suggested to him that he put his injured left arm through the open window. He actually agreed thinking there was a sound reason for it, probably thinking in first aid terms.

"Yes there was a reason," I replied, telling him that I did not want him bleeding inside my car! He was not impressed but I got him to hospital where he was looked after.

I remember going into the Queens Pub in Talbot Road with a Detective Sergeant, as we walked in I noticed a group of lads at a table. One of them started to barrack us, I bristled at this and said we ought to have words. The sergeant told me to leave it and have a drink. As we walked out of the pub the sergeant walked up to the lad, shook his hand and said, "Thanks a lot". He released the lad's hand and walked way. The lad opened his hand to find a ten shilling note. His mates then started to question him why a detective should give him money. Fred winked at me and said,

"There's more than one way to deal with them". I thought maybe so, but I could not afford to give ten bob notes to yobbos.

We used to go into RHO Hills and have coffee, meet the store detectives and General Manager John Stewart. I was looking for a radio and John Stewart suggested I take one and try it. I borrowed a B & O transistor radio. During the trial period on 7 May 1967 there was a huge fire which destroyed much of the building. I went to the store two months later and they were using accommodation next to the damaged part of the store. I returned the radio I had on loan much to the surprise of the salesman who received it. I still have the receipt dated 7.7.67.

We often got visiting police officers, usually from the UK, however, on one occasion we had to look after four Zambian Detectives. They had met Detective Inspector John Brown whilst attending a course in Wakefield and he had arranged for the officers to visit Blackpool during the Easter Weekend in April 1968. We arranged for them to stay at a guest house adjoining South Shore Police Station run by the lovely Mrs Bamford. They enjoyed their stay there. The officers were Detective Inspectors Anderson Munamonga, Charles Mbao, Bradlow Nyundu and Evans Njovu. Although the same rank, Anderson seemed to take the lead. We took them to the top of Blackpool Tower, Blackpool Pleasure Beach and on Easter Monday (15 April) to see the football match at Bloomfield Road between Blackpool and Blackburn Rovers.

They certainly enjoyed their visit and one of them asked if we could get him a fishing net. We took them to a fancy goods shop and selected one. However, what he required was a large trawl net to use on a boat on one of the large lakes in Zambia!

Working in Blackpool meant that from time to time you came into contact with well-known entertainers. Having had a couple of thefts to deal with (one being the theft of large feathers used by the lady dancers) from the Queens Theatre, I used to pop in occasionally and have a chat and drink with the manager Archie

Stewart. Tommy Cooper came into the bar and Archie introduced me. Tommy said that he had lost a nice pen. I told him we had a lost property office and he could visit to see as we had many pens handed in. Tommy said that he was not bothered about getting the original one back, if there was another nice one in the property office. When he went Archie said, "You thought he was joking, he wasn't".

A colleague and I got called to the North Pier one day. Apparently, there had been thefts from the artistes' dressing rooms. We met the pier manager and the manager for the company producing the show. The company manager was a Londoner who was really 'steaming' about the lack of security and the fact that the stars of the show had suffered losses. Unfortunately, it was not just the two of us that could hear him but anyone within a reasonable distance.

The case was allocated to me. The company manager asked if we were going to question any of the pier staff.

"Not now," I said, "You have alerted everyone"!

I told my colleague that we would investigate but would let the 'dust settle'. A very expensive bottle of aftershave had been stolen from the dressing room of the popular Scottish entertainer, Andy Stewart. We obtained details of the cleaners etc. from the pier manager. Two or three weeks later, we went to a flat occupied by one of the cleaners. He opened the door; I breathed in and sniffed and told him he was being arrested for theft. He was wearing the stolen aftershave!

After the court case we went back to the pier. We had recovered other property and we returned the aftershave and a golf sweater to Andy Stewart. He had not noticed the sweater was missing, he enquired if there was anything else. We said "No". He thanked us and we left.

We then called on the Star of the Show, Dickie Henderson, we had only recovered some of his socks. He was so pleased the thefts had been cleared up and he invited us into his dressing room and we all had a drink. He was a charming man.

In 1964 the Beatles were in Blackpool for the Sunday Night Shows at the ABC Theatre in Church Street. They were mobbed by adoring fans wherever they went and Blackpool was no exception. They were staying at the Imperial Hotel and the Chief Constable decided that they would receive 24-hour protection. I was on the day shift with an experienced detective, Norman Brown. We stood guard outside their room and chatted to them. We then had to escort their vehicle to the ABC. The Chief Constable was outside the Imperial. I was driving my white Morris Minor thousand and he waved me on. We went to the ABC and the Beatles were rehearsing.

I seem to recall the TV producer was called Philip Jones or similar. He was certainly getting exasperated with the lads and I heard this voice over the speaker system telling them to stop messing about and play something. I could not help but smile when they started playing 'Needles and Pins' the number one UK hit record for The Searches.

One case allocated to me involved an alleged assault on Con Cluskey, from The Bachelors singing group. They were appearing at The Central Pier whose top of the bill was Al Read a very popular comedian. The Bachelors' record 'Diane' had reached the number one spot. It was a record breaking season very much due to their popularity. The boys had rented a house on West Park Drive, Blackpool for the summer season that was owned by a local bookie. One night the owner went to the house to check and an altercation took place. Con alleged that the owner had assaulted him. I had to interview all the witnesses and the house owner, who denied the assault. There was sufficient evidence for a trial which took place at Blackpool Quarter Sessions, held at the Town Hall and presided over by Deputy Recorder, Judge John Corcoran.

I had to obtain a list of witness expenses, a waste of time really in respect of Con and Dec Cluskey. There was no way the courts would pay what they earned! We had a break and they wanted a coffee, the prosecuting barrister told me to go with them and not let them out of my sight. I had to ensure we got them all back into court. We went into Collinson's Cafe in Market Street. It was quite a big group that ordered, and I realised that it would be a hefty bill. No one offered to pay and I said, "Don't look at me, I'm not paying"! One of the friends paid. At the conclusion of the trial, the house owner was acquitted.

When I was at South CID Office, I went with a Detective Sergeant to a burglary at Ramsden's Tobacconist in Waterloo Road. It was an interesting case because the burglars must have taken inspiration from the acclaimed 1955 French film *Rififi* where burglars had broken into a jewellers' shop by drilling through the shop ceiling from an apartment directly above. The same modus operandi had been used.

We started to make enquiries and spoke to the occupier of a flat on the first floor. He was an 84-year-old newspaper seller. He assured us he had not seen or heard anything suspicious. I thanked him and said we would call back later to see if he had remembered anything. He asked why it was necessary and I explained he might remember or hear something after we had gone. He seemed uncomfortable so I asked if there was a problem.

He responded by saying, "It won't be a Thursday night when you come back, will it?"

I asked what the significance of Thursday was.

"My girlfriend comes on that night," he said.

Being a cheeky young detective I said, "Well if we come back, we won't be disturbing anything at your age".

"You cheeky bugger," he said, "She is only in her sixties and if I don't perform, she'll accused me of having another woman!"

I asked, "What's your secret then?"

He said, "Do you really want to know?" and I told him I did. He went to a large old fashioned sideboard. He opened both doors and it was full of tins of rice pudding. He told me that he had a tin of rice pudding every day! You learn something new every day.

April 1969 saw the County Borough of Blackpool Borough Police amalgamate with Lancashire Constabulary and I was transferred to the No1 District Task Force CID.

When Darren was about 7-years-old he was having difficulty with fractions, and these were simple fractions. So I thought he needed a practical example. I took hold of two oranges and cut one into quarters and left one whole.

I said, "Look Darren," holding the whole orange. "This is a whole one".

I put the four quarters together, and said, "Together, they are a whole one," then holding two quarters together continued, "These two quarters make a half, and one piece is a quarter".

Time and time again I went through the routine but he never grasped it. To my shame I became frustrated and eventually lost my temper flinging the whole orange to the floor landing near to Darren's feet. Fortunately it hit the floor not him, although Darren's recollection is that it caught him! We have often laughed about that. It was however a defining moment and proved one thing; I could never become a teacher!

Constable Jeffrey Meadows

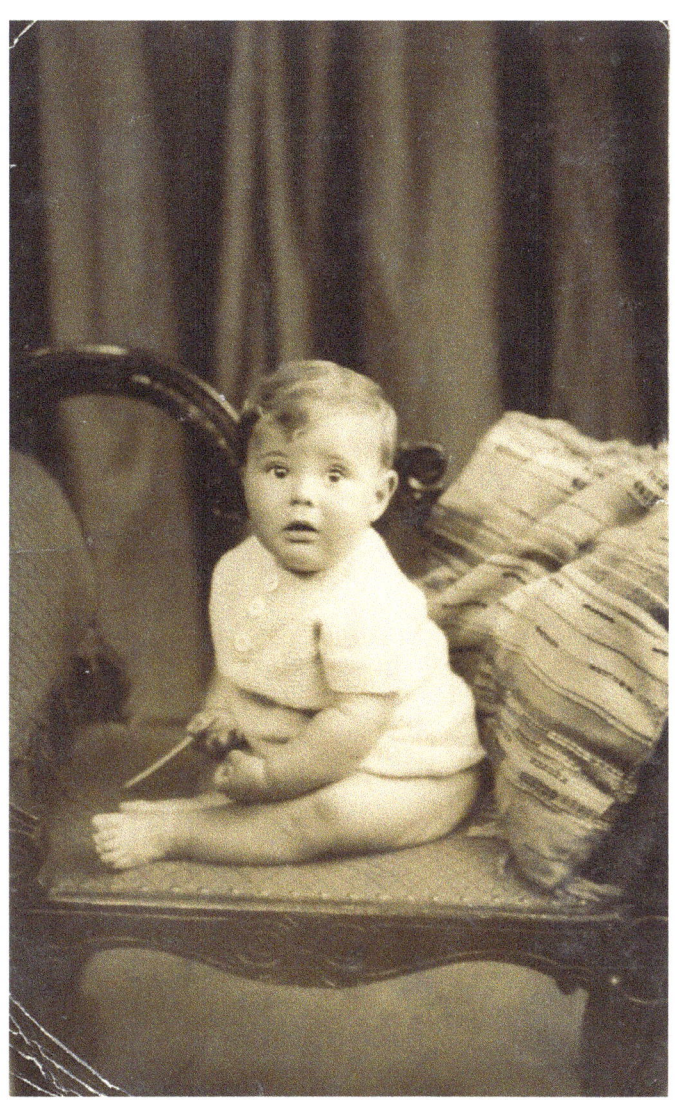

Baby Jeffrey Meadows

Julia with Jim, John & Jeff Meadows

The boys in 2008

The Meadows' at Penrose

Jeff and ER board

Highfield school play

Jeff at Co-op butchers Harrowside

Young Kathy

Strolling on the Prom

BLACKPOOL COUNTY
BOROUGH POLICE FORCE.

DECLARATION.

I, JEFFREY MEADOWS,

do solemnly and sincerely declare that I will well and truly serve our Sovereign Lady the Queen, in the office of a Borough Constable for the County Borough of Blackpool.

I will execute all precepts and warrants to me directed, and do all other matters pertaining to and things relating to my office according to the best of my skill and ability, and without any manner of partiality.

J Meadows
P.C. 189

Made and subscribed before
me at Blackpool this **5th**
day of **October,** 1957.

William Pomfrit

A Justice having jurisdiction in the Borough.

Beat Book

No. 7 Beat.

Commence beat at corner Newhouse Road and Preston New Road. Newhouse Road to Johnson Road, back to Waterloo Road, Waterloo Road south side, Rectory Road, Ilford Road (Acton Road alternately), Arnott Road, Hawes Side Lane to Police Station. ($\frac{1}{2}$ hour).

Crossland Road, Vicarage Lane, Angers Hill Road, Ryson Avenue, Penrose Avenue, James Avenue, Newhouse Road, Barclay Avenue to corner of Preston New Road. (1 hour)

Briercliffe Avenue, Preston Old Road, Royal Bank Road, Lindsay Avenue, (Airedale Avenue alternately), Beechfield Avenue, West Park Drive, Kenwyn Avenue, Knowsley Avenue to West Park Drive. ($1\frac{1}{2}$ hours)

Knowsley Avenue, Kempton Avenue (Vernon Avenue alternately), Beechfield Avenue, Whitegate Drive east side, Honister Avenue, South Park Drive, Preston New Road to corner of Newhouse Road. (2 hours)

<u>ALL STREETS AND PROPERTY ABUTTING THERETO.</u>

Seven Beat

John & Julia Meadows

Kathleen and Jeff's wedding day

Kathy in honeymoon caravan

Family Group

First car

Mrs PC 189

Four Zambian Detective Inspectors

Hydrangea Banner

Marton United Glamour line up

Jeff chatting to football supporters

Jeff at Bloomfield Road

sented annually within the division for outstanding service by the Specials.

Communication.

Overheard on the radio—' South to P.C. ... Go to this address. The householder has had an egg thrown at her window, she is eggs-asperated'. Reply: 'You must be yolking'. Another P.C., interposing, ' Do you mind unscrambling that message '.

P.C. at a rural station took a simple message from the owner of a dog which was lost. He believed that the man had lost an expensive two-hour dog, of which he was very fond. On reflection later he wondered what sort of dog this was, and it took some time to discover it was a Chihuahua dog.

A man climbed through an open bedroom window, asked complainant for money, stole contents from purse then threw £5 on to the bed saying, ' That is from the cat '. He also wrote the words ' The Cat ' on a mirror in lipstick. When he was dealt with he asked for 13 offences to be taken into consideration—10 of which were for stealing bottles of milk—one pint at a time—CAN YOU LICK THAT?

In a Central League match played at Bloomfield Road on 9th February, 1971, between Blackpool Reserves and Burnley Reserves the two linesmen were P.C.'s. 3831 David Taylor of CG Section and 3821 Derek Taylor of HQ/TP. Both of these men are active participants in the divisional football team and in their spare time actively participate in the running of local club matches. Incidentally the game was won by Blackpool Reserves by one goal to nil—biased? never!

'**Moses**' **at Bloomfield Road**—a true story in the every day life of a bunch of lawmen and their leader, Moses, in controlling the Philistines.

The drawing appeared on the notice board at District Headquarters masterminded by one of the Task Force personnel who was on duty on the day in question. The incident was the Blackpool v. Huddersfield football match at Bloomfield Road, Blackpool, in October last year, when the unruly mobs came face to face with the law in the shape of Jeff (Moses) Meadows and his flock—the drawing, some say, accurately depicts the scene after the match. On a serious note though after the match large numbers of youths rampaged through the Blackpool streets terrifying members of the public. Members of the No. 1 District Task Force deployed in the area went into action and to quote the words of one of the magistrates, ' restored law and order to the town '. No fewer than 69 youths and girls were subsequently arrested and of this number only four pleaded guilty. The majority of the not guilty pleas were represented by barristers and solicitors and the proceedings were heard in eight separate Magistrates' Courts resulting in all but two being proven guilty.

One part of Sergeant Meadows evidence was that he alone faced a screaming, menacing crowd of 200 plus youngsters and was likened to by the defence as ' Canute trying to turn back the waves ' and ' Moses ' trying to part the

sea '. When another officer was asked why he together with another dog handler could not stop the crowds, he replied that he would require rubber extending arms to cross the 40 foot wide road. The cases were naturally prosecuted for convictions but even through the seriousness of the job, humour frequently arose as can be seen from some of the extracts. Well done lads.

PRESTON (D) DIVISION
David Best.

It always seems to be a difficult task when sitting down to write the quarterly notes for the Journal, to find material in sufficient quantity to make it worthwhile and readable at the same time but truly, this must be one of the leanest quarters I have known. Nevertheless, I will throw caution to the winds so to speak and try and entertain you as best I can.

First of all, storytime. One afternoon, two members of the plain clothes department at Preston called at a local Indian Restaurant with the intention of using one of the upstairs rooms for observation purposes. The owner of the restaurant had given them similar permission on previous occasions but on this particular day he was absent and upon entering the premises they were met by a young Pakistani waiter who did not know who they were. The conversation, which has a nightmarish quality about it, went as follows:—

Police officer: Good afternoon.

Pakistani: (Who spoke very little English) Pardon ?

Jeff Moses facing the crowd

Jeff with Maggie Thatcher Blackpool

Jeff with colleagues holding back protesters at Winter Gardens

Inspector Jeffrey with stick

Jeff with pupils at Bamber Bridge

From Albert Laugharne, Q.P.M.   Chief Constable.

POLICE HEADQUARTERS
HUTTON, PRESTON, PR4 5SB

TELEPHONE: LONGTON 614444
TELEX: 67619 and 67610 LANCON

TO WHOM IT MAY CONCERN

I, Albert Laugharne, Chief Constable of the Lancashire Constabulary, have the honour to introduce the bearers of this document, Jeffrey Meadows, a Detective Chief Inspector and Alan William Taylor, a Detective Inspector in the Lancashire Constabulary.

These officers are engaged on my behalf in enquiring into the recent murder in this county of Christopher Martin Johnstone, a New Zealand citizen, and related matters which involve the activities of a large scale criminal drug smuggling and distribution network.

I shall be most grateful for any assistance that you are able to afford my officers to facilitate their enquiries.

Laugharne.

9th November 1979

CHAPTER EIGHT
PROMOTION TO SERGEANT

On a couple of occasions I sat the examination for promotion to Sergeant. I failed but it was not surprising because I had not done any preparation. If I am being honest, I was enjoying life in CID and loved being a detective. Eventually, you get an attack of common sense and I saw people being promoted and I thought that I should put myself in a position where I could be considered, so during my eleventh year of service, I decided I should sit the examination which was set by the Civil Service Commission.

The Division ran courses for those wishing to take the exams. My colleague Ross Jewitt and I enrolled. You had to attend the classes in your own time. It was so worthwhile, one of the problems was that when answering a question, one tended to assume that basic knowledge was not required, as the examiner would accept that the person taking the examination would have that basic knowledge.

One lesson we learned was that we should treat the examiner as 'an idiot child'. For example, in the Traffic Paper, when answering a question about vehicles displaying lights during hours of darkness, you had to state, "the vehicle should be parked with its nearside next to the kerb". Common sense really.

Well we passed the sergeant's exam, at that time, once you passed the examination for promotion to sergeant, you were allowed to sit the Inspector's examination. The problem was that time was short but I thought, "In for a penny, in for a pound". So with a little extra revision I sat the examination and passed. Not only did I pass but I was in the top 200 nationally. Had I been younger, I could have applied for an interview for the Special Course.

As it stood, I was one of only three Detective Constables in Lancashire Constabulary qualified for promotion to Inspector. That must have worked in my favour because in August 1969, I was promoted to uniform sergeant based at Blackpool Central.

During July every year Blackpool played host to a multitude of Glaswegians who came to celebrate Glasgow Fair. They also came for a weekend in the Illuminations period from Friday evening until Monday morning. Many would leave from Blackpool North Railway Station at lunchtime on the Monday.

I first came across the impact of Glasgow Fair when I was a young constable. I was in company of a probationary constable. A crowd had gathered on the promenade embankment by the Open Air Baths on South Promenade. We estimated that the crowd numbered in excess of 200 people. A couple of revellers were playing the accordion and the crowd were having a good time. Large crowds were not encouraged. My colleague said, "Let's go and break them up".

Discretion being the better part of valour, I urged caution. A little later some idiot started to throw fireworks. Now was the time to act. I sussed out one of the 'leaders'. I went to him and said that whilst they had been having a good time, some idiot had spoiled it for them and it was time to disperse. The man I spoke to said, "OK, we'll finish this song and go".

After the song the crowd just evaporated. On other occasions I had seen the singing Scottish revellers in such numbers that they completely blocked Albert Road, a road which gave access to the town centre.

Scottish detectives would travel down to identify known troublemakers and whilst the majority of Scots were content to have a good time there were some pretty bad Glaswegians.

One Monday morning together with a Detective Sergeant, we walked into the top bar of the Palatine Hotel on Central

Promenade. It was 'bursting at the seams', many of them were young Scots and as we walked in it went quiet. Then in unison they all started to sing, "You can stick Blackpool Tower up your arse!" This was not a good sign. On that morning there had been several stabbings when the offenders chased their victims from the Promenade and through a boarding house before stabbing their prey.

The nature of the crimes changed from year to year. One year it would be stabbings; another it was grievous bodily harm (a favourite weapon being a potato with razor blades inserted). Then there would be smash and grabs, burglaries and thefts from the person. We were kept busy.

When they were arriving at North Railway Station we would be there with the white police land rover parked on the concourse to welcome them. We were also there when they returned to the train station. I was there as a uniform sergeant on one occasion accompanied by a Detective Inspector. The force policy was that any Inspector who had completed the three-year Lancaster University Course was appointed Detective Inspector, notwithstanding that many had no previous CID experience.

The Glaswegians started to return to the station. I caught sight of one youth and shouted to one of the PC's to arrest him. The Detective Inspector said, "Why is he being arrested Sergeant"?

"For theft," I replied.

His next question was "But where is your evidence"?

I looked at him and said, "I know of no jeweller who would sell the pad with all the rings on"! He had not noticed the tray of rings. This was the Detective Inspector who sometime later referred to me as a 'Chief Constable's Nightmare'. It was when on the Task Force, my team often locked up large groups of troublemakers. As you will hear later, on one afternoon and evening we arrested

101 troublemakers. Incidents like that probably reinforced his view that I was indeed 'A Chief Constable's Nightmare"!

The sea can be very cruel; one night I was called to the Promenade, just south of the North Pier. Crowds were lining the railings and two constables were stripping off. I asked them what they were doing and they said that a man was in the sea and they were going in to assist him. I asked them to show me where the man was. We looked and could not see him; all we could see was the 'white horses' on the waves. I told the lads to get dressed. We used a powerful lamp to scan the waves. The inshore lifeboat was being launched. The crowds were shouting that the man was in the water. I told them that I believed them but until we could see the man, I was not risking the lives of the two officers. The man was not traced that night and sadly his body was washed up at South Shore the next morning. I asked the officers when they last swum. One could not remember and one last swum on his holidays some months before. We could well have lost two officers that night and it was a lesson that rank demands responsible leadership.

One of the talks I give is called 'Lessons Learned' and I talk about experiences in the job, many of which are lighthearted. One of the lessons I learned was that you did not win against barrister Richard Henriques as a rule. I did get the better of him on one occasion when I was a uniform sergeant, a burglary had occurred in the Grasmere Road area. We traced the offenders and they were locked up. I interviewed the main offender who was not the easiest to deal with, however, when we got to court he pleaded guilty which meant I could sit in court whilst the other offenders were dealt with. Mr Henriques was representing one of them and his defence was that he was drunk and was not capable. I had seen this man getting dressed. I passed a note to the prosecuting barrister Mr Fairclough who got permission to call me into the witness box.

I told the Court that I had seen him putting his socks on and to do so, he stood on one leg and was in no way unsteady. Looking at the jury Mr Henriques asked me if I would have breathalysed the man if I had come across him.

I said, "No Sir".

"You would not breathalyse him; tell the jury sergeant why you would not breathalyse him".

"Because Sir, we do not breathalyse pedestrians", I replied.

He tried to carry on with that line of questioning but Judge Corcoran stopped him. The lesson there was cherish the moment because there would not be too many of them with Richard Henriques! (However, he did me a favour when I was a detective sergeant. I had been talking to two of my detective constables about the quality of evidence. They obviously did not listen because they came back from Preston Crown Court muttering away because they had lost their case. I asked them what went wrong and they rather begrudgingly told me that Mr Henriques had told them that when giving evidence, they should dot their 'i's' and cross their 't's' like Sergeant Meadows. They had not taken notice of what I had said but thereafter they would certainly take notice of what Mr Henriques' told them).

After seven months as a section sergeant, I transferred as sergeant on the Uniformed Crime Patrol (Z Cars) of the No 1 District Task Force (DTF). The DTF comprised of uniformed crime patrols officers, dog handlers and a CID contingent who investigated serious crimes e.g. murder. Sergeant Bob Dobson had encouraged me to join the Task Force. This was also when I met Linda Cawley daughter of Superintendent Harold Cawley. Linda typed many of my voluminous reports when we arrested football hooligans etc. She did not have it any easier when I returned to Task Force some years later as Detective Chief Inspector because we dealt with some serious cases with large files! Later she was the Divisional Chief Superintendent's PA.

No 1 District had its own Assistant Chief Constable Tom Watkinson, he did not like my sideburns which he referred to as 'louse ladders'. He asked what would make me trim them. I said that he could have an inch off the sideburns if I got a driving course. Well I got my driving course and trimmed the 'louse ladders' by one inch.

No 1 DTF covered three divisions, 'A' Division covered parts of what is now Cumbria Constabulary, e.g. Barrow, Ulverston, Coniston, Hawkshead and parts of old Westmorland. 'B' Division covered the Lancaster, Morecambe and Garstang areas. 'C' Division covered Blackpool, Fleetwood, St Anne's and the north and south Fylde areas.

The District Task Force Commander was the District Detective Superintendent, the senior CID Officer in No 1 DTF. His Deputy was a Detective Chief Inspector who in addition being involved in criminal investigation also had responsibility for the large uniform group.

Many of the crime patrol were seasoned officers. They were of course based at different police stations but often came into our HQ at Bispham Police Office for refreshment. Some liked to play cards usually for matches, but I suspected that money was changing hands. It never happened when I was there so I addressed them all and said I did not want them playing for money; family men could not afford to lose their money playing cards. One old sweat told me that what they did in their own time was a matter for them and I could not do anything about it. When they all paraded at the beginning of their shifts the next night, I allocated their refreshment times but sent each to their home station e.g. St Annes, Blackpool or Fleetwood. That really shocked them and I looked at the old sweat and said, "Now tell me, I cannot do anything about it". When I did let them eat together, they played cards but not for money.

On one occasion No 1 District Task Force officers were deployed to prevent trouble at a Blackpool Football Club match.

I was briefing the officers when I espied a man who I knew was wanted on warrant. We had been joined by members of No 2 District Task Force. I shouted to one of my team (No 1DTF) to arrest the man. The visiting officers from No 2 DTF were, to say the least puzzled and perhaps unsettled, thinking we just arrested anyone walking by. We did put them wise!

On 23 August 1971, Superintendent Gerald Richardson from Blackpool DHQ was gunned down following an armed raid at a town centre jewellers. A major man hunt followed. At the time I was on holiday. On my return, the culprits had been arrested. On my first day back from leave, Detective Inspector Roy Eglon took me down to the Home Office Scientific Branch at Crewe where we took possession of a quantity of the very latest metal detectors.

What followed was a six week search along the A6 road from Carnforth to Tebay. I was on the search every day that I was on duty together with one of my fellow sergeants. Frederick Sewell had apparently told interviewing officers that he had thrown a handgun away on that stretch of the A6. I briefed the team every day and told them that they had to search from the nearside of the road to a distance which would be appropriate. I told them to think Sewell could throw like an Olympian.

At the conclusion of the day it was very evident where we had searched with rubbish in piles. One day the lads were standing by a fence. They did not want to go in the field because there was a bull in there. My brother John, a farmer had a bull. I told them not to be wimps and climbed over the fence and walked to the limit of the search area and told them to come in. They did and completed the search area. The bull remained at the far end of the field. It is a fine line between encouragement and foolhardiness.

On one occasion when they were having a meal break I caught a couple of them up a tree collecting conkers!

On the day we finished the search we were in the hills near Tebay. It was cold and we were visited by a true legend, Assistant

Chief Constable Joe Mounsey. Joe had been a key player in the Moors Murder enquiry. We were due a lunchbreak so we went into a nearby pub where he bought the lads a drink, "I'm spending the coal money," he said jokingly.

Joe, Jack a fellow sergeant and I ordered a bar meal. A nice hot meal arrived, Joe looked round and commented that none of the lads were eating and he felt bad that we were. I told him not to worry, I told him that as soon as he left, their butties would come out and, of course they could claim their subsistence allowance. Joe was happy to eat his lunch then!

We never did find the gun and Sewell and his gang were convicted. Sewell served 30 years and it is said that he made a million pounds whilst in prison through property deals.

Resulting from that fateful day, there was nine gallantry awards, an unprecedented number of awards from a single incident:

George Cross
Superintendent Gerald Irving Richardson (posthumously)
Constable Carl Walker

George Medal
Constable Ian Hampson
Constable Andrew Hillis
Constable Patrick Jackson
Sergeant Kenneth Mackay

British Empire Medal for Gallantry
Inspector Edward Gray
Constable Edward Hanley

Queen's Commendation for Brave Conduct
Inspector Stephen Drummond Redpath

Of those nine officers, sadly only retired Chief Superintendent Kenneth Mackay, retired Inspector Carl Walker and retired

Sergeant Ian Hampson are with us today. Ian Hampson was one of the constables I prevented from going into the sea when I was a sergeant (page 103).

The above were all very worthy winners of the gallantry awards. There were other acts of bravery that day. According to reports, Blackpool Fireman Ronald Gale, who was in uniform was passing the shop on that fateful day. He saw what was happening and asked a couple to phone the police. Ron walked into the shop doorway to be confronted by one of the robbers Frederick Sewell who was armed with a shotgun, which he pushed forcibly into Ron Gale's stomach. Ron grabbed the barrel but was hit over the head with an iron bar falling unconscious in the doorway. A window cleaner, Malcolm Sarjantson chased the robbers into Queens Square. It seems a shame that Ron and Malcolm did not receive a similar gallantry award

As a task force sergeant you had responsibility for crime patrol officers and dog handlers in three divisions. This meant that you covered A, B and C Divisions. We worked a five week rota of 10am to 6pm and 8pm to 4am. Two weeks of that rota was working the 8pm to 4am shift. Of course, if circumstances demanded it, shifts were often changed.

Once, when on the late shift (8pm to 4am), I was supervising patrols in the A and B Divisions. When I was in the Morecambe area, I radioed for the position of one of the B Division crime patrol cars. "White Lund Estate," was the reply. I went to the main access/exit point and waited for them. And then I toured the industrial estate. There was no sign of the crime car. I later spoke to the two officers and immediately, the older and more senior of the two, "Did you check both ways in and out Sarge"?

I replied that I had.

"Ah, he said. There are actually three ways in and out".

The sergeants would alternate working A and B Divisions or the C Division. The next night I was due to work C Division. I changed with my fellow sergeant and I went back up to B Division and spent some time on White Lund Estate. I actually found at least four ways in and out of White Lund Estate. I spoke to the officers and the older officer tried to come up with some excuse but I warned them that any more nonsense would result in serious consequences!

I had to go to an incident involving the same officer, I was riding in a dog van (not my favourite pastime!) when we received a call to White Lund Estate. Travellers often parked there and the officer who had deliberately misled me about the access to the estate was there. He was investigating a theft of some carpet and was doing a lot of shouting and he had called for assistance.

The dog handler was a competent and sound officer and we both agreed the situation could turn nasty. The officer who called for assistance was arguing with an older man who was clearly the leader of the travellers. I asked for a situation report and the officer said he intended to search the leader's caravan. He said we needed more officers. The leader was adamant he was not going to allow that. We noticed that about 20 or 30 strapping young men had gathered.

Our crime patrol officer was not trying to reduce the tension, but seem intent on stirring it up, I told him to be quiet and keep his mouth shut. I took the leader to one side and I told him that we were both in a difficult position. I said words to the effect, "You need to keep face with your people and you must know that there is no way I can leave without your caravan being searched. I could call for the cavalry but people on both sides could get hurt. Would you let me search your van?" He agreed and I searched the van with him present. There was no carpet hidden and we shook hands and left. My problem was that I could not rely entirely on what the officer had said. I later spoke to him and in the official jargon, "Gave him words of advice".

Ulverston is a nice market town in the South Lakes. I was told to go there and meet the Chief Inspector concerning some problems. At night time, the local Bobby was having hard time with some troublemakers. I was asked if I could take the Task Force up there to support the Bobby and send out a message that there was plenty of support for the local Bobbies. So one evening I went to Ulverston with four crime cars and two dog vans. We identified the ring leader of the troublemakers – everywhere he went, there was a uniformed task force member or dog handler nearby. As he went from pub to pub, he was under close but silent observation, he certainly got the message because he was heard to ask one of the elderly regulars to walk him home. Apparently, he felt that he could end up in the police station if he was on his own. The Chief Inspector was delighted, we had not arrested anyone and had not caused mayhem. The troublemakers had got the message and peace was restored.

The crime patrol was very good at restoring order. On one occasion we were called to Talbot Square in Blackpool. Crowds thronged the square and a coach had stopped and the drunken male passengers had alighted and were causing trouble. Section officers were struggling to contain the situation and several crime patrol cars arrived. Crime patrol officers could be readily identified with their flat caps and short gabardine car coats. They did help to restore order quite quickly. Much to my surprise, there was a spontaneous round of applause from the large crowd who had witnessed the incident.

Yobbish behaviour was a problem, not least with some football supporters, there was a tendency after the match for some to rampage through Blackpool Town Centre. Anticipating trouble on the day of one match, I briefed the Task Officers and deployed them to strategic points. I told the officers that if there was a rampaging mob, they should be arrested. These mobs used to chant and I told the officers that they must not surmise who was shouting or guess. It would be very difficult to attribute particular chants to individuals. Providing they could be identified as running with the mob, they should be arrested. That would be our case which we would put to the magistrates.

Well it happened at a Blackpool versus Huddersfield match. We also had to deal with a separate mob in the evening. In all 101 people were arrested. 95 pleaded not guilty and there followed several weeks of court appearances. Of the 95 who pleaded 'Not Guilty', 93 were convicted and the Task Force team was congratulated by the justices for restoring order to the town.

As Task Force officers, we took the issue of public disorder seriously and we regularly made large group arrests e.g. in excess of 20 or 30. It seems that our activities may have caused some concern to senior officers. One of my Inspectors had a quiet word with me. He told me that the Inspectors and other senior officers were told to monitor the arrests by my team. It seemed that others may have also seen me as a 'Chief Constable's nightmare'!

On one occasion, I was joined on patrol by a uniformed Superintendent, it could not have worked out better. It was an evening match and after the match, I patrolled the area close to the football ground. As we drove north along Lytham Road towards the Promenade, we saw a large gang of rampaging youths. As they ran they smashed plate glass shop windows. I was driving so I followed the youths onto the central coach park and saw them run onto a coach. I went onto the coach and told the driver to identify the group members who had just run onto the coach. It was not difficult for him because there had only been a couple or so passengers on before the group joined them. I arrested them all, an action the Superintendent agreed with.

At their court appearance some were acquitted. The Superintendent had provided a statement but was unable to attend court for the trial. It may be that we would have convicted more had he given evidence. Interestingly, no other senior officer accompanied me thereafter when I was on anti-public disorder patrol. Perhaps they were satisfied with the way I operated.

There was an amusing side to it, Superintendent Gerry Richardson who was not the Superintendent referred to above, said to me that he was changing the name of my Task Force Team. He said they would be known as 'Meadows' Gorillas' named after *'Garrison's Gorillas'* the ABC TV series broadcast from 1967 to 1968, which was about a mixed bunch of Second World War Commandos!

It was not just the antics of the supporters which could be offensive. One night, when in company with a dog handler we were travelling along the Parade Embankment and in a tram shelter saw a professional footballer in a comprising position with a young lady. After strong words from us he was very apologetic and was given a verbal warning. One of the considerations to take into account was that on a busy night, trouble could break out and your colleague may need speedy back up. Therefore, you would not want to tie yourself up in a charge office when a strong verbal warning would be effective.

The Cherry Tree Hotel (now demolished) at Marton was a very busy pub. It attracted many visitors as well as residents. We were parked up one night and there was a coach nearby. The driver was waiting for his passengers to come back. We saw one chap with a full tray of meat pies, he was carrying them on his head. Ted Swindlehurst, the lad I was with got out, spoke to him and ascertained he had not purchased the pies. We didn't think he had because they were in a large metal tray. Ted arrested the lad, seated him in the car and took the tray of pies back into the pub so that they could be kept fresh and safe. Then a gang of lads who were walking back to the coach, saw the prisoner and told us they were going to release him and take him onto the coach. A big fellow amongst them started to walk round with his hands in the air shouting, "Lancashire Constabulary are bastards!"

Now we can be pretty sharp at times, so I called for backup. Several Crime Patrol cars and a couple of dog vans arrived promptly, which was just as well because a full scale mêlée was playing out.

It wasn't easy to restore order and I looked to see two dog handlers standing idly by. I bellowed at them, "Don't stand there with your brains in neutral," whereupon one dog handler came behind me and a yob kicked the dog and it went for the nearest person, me! It sank its teeth into my backside and I could feel the blood draining from my face. My words to the dog handler are not printable. It finished up with us shepherding all the lads who were fighting onto the empty coach and taking them all to Central Police Office where they were duly charged with disorderly behaviour.

I had to go to Blackpool Victoria Hospital when things went quiet to get a tetanus injection. I was a little suspicious when I got there and told the nurse I would have the injection in my arm. Just as well because some of the crime patrol officers and dog handlers turned up – they were out of sight – waiting for me to drop my trousers for the jab. They were sorely disappointed. I once got bitten at another incident and it made me realise that the police dogs did not know the difference between 'goodies' and 'baddies'!

Ted Swindlehurst was a good Bobby, sadly, he died in his late 40's. He and his partner Ed Jacobs were great thief-takers. They brought me back from Barrow Police Station one night. This was before the improvements to the A590 and the journey from Barrow to Bispham took just 60 minutes! Ed, a first class police advanced driver was at the wheel and they commented that it was the first time they have never heard me chat in the car!

One of the crime patrol officers was rather boastful one night, he said that if he did not have a prisoner that night he would 'show his bare arse in Talbot Square'. Just before the end of our shift at 2am, I called for all the cars to rendezvous with me for a debrief at Talbot Square. All the patrols turned up except for one car. No prizes for guessing which officer failed to turn up in Talbot Square.

My next move was to Central CID Office where I remained for about three years. On one occasion we arrested two men after information that they were in possession of gelignite. Forensic evidence was gathered. One of the defendants escaped going to court after it was accepted (by the lawyers, not the detectives) that traces of the gelignite found came from the clothing of the co-accused. The inevitable happened, when the remaining accused appeared at court, his defence was that his clothing could have been contaminated from gelignite from the clothing of the man who was released! He was acquitted.

The forensic scientist was convinced that he had handled explosive material. Before he was released, and as he could not be recharged, he subsequently agreed to show us where he had hidden the gelignite. He told us that he had hidden the gelignite under the North Pier. He agreed to see if it could be recovered. We approached from the south side and he pointed up to the top of the vertical stanchions. He said it was just under the walk way and he volunteered to climb up and it was astounding to witness how he shinned up the iron legs and within minutes was at the top. There was no trace of the gelignite and we were never able to determine whether it had actually been there.

Being a seaside resort brought its own problems for gullible holidaymakers. Mock Auctions operated on the Golden Mile. The 'auctioneers' would invite passers-by into their saleroom. Once a reasonable crowd was in they would close the doors restricting entry to others. They would sell many articles such as electrical goods (which were often bought from sellers in Bury New Road, Manchester). We classed them as Mock Auctions because the operators engaged in Dutch bidding where the price decreases to a level acceptable to the 'auctioneer'. They were good spielers and the crowd would be spellbound. The problem was that after members of the public took possession of their goods they realised that what they had often paid large sums for were not what they expected.

The modus operandi of the so called salesmen meant that at the beginning of the sale, one person would get a really good bargain. Would-be buyers were beguiled and fell into the trap of thinking they were getting the bargain, their desire fuelled by greed and their own vulnerability.

We received many complaints so the Detective Superintendent told us to go and take some action. Three or four of us went down to the main saleroom. We gained entry and having identified ourselves shouted to the 'auctioneer' to stop the sale. What happened next was astounding, some members of the crowd turned on us accusing us of being part of the Mock Auction Team! In the confusion that followed, the 'auctioneer' and his mates slipped out through the back. They were traced later but evidence was lost. The Mock Auction team employed competent solicitors and it's sad to say the Mock Auctions carried on. When I was a Uniform Inspector I had to deal with this scourge again but more of that later.

One night I popped into the Gaiety Bar on Market Street in the Town Centre. I was in the quiet area when a member of the staff said there was some trouble in the main bar. I went into the main bar area where a young chap was quite distressed. He and his mate, both from down south had been to a football match in Manchester then came to Blackpool where they stayed overnight. Apparently, they did this quite often. A young footballer was out with his father and some friends when there had been some sort of dispute and the young visitor had been assaulted.

The father of the footballer did not help and he was 'mouthing off'. From the enquiries I made, it seemed that the lad who had been assaulted was the innocent party. I called for the night CID crew and they arrived and started to chat to the young footballer. The detectives, who were both tall men, were stood with their backs to the entrance, facing the footballer and I was behind the footballer slightly to the side. The next thing I saw a glint of metal and the footballer was struck on the head. The lad who had been assaulted had slipped outside and had picked up a piece of scaffolding tubing (there was outside building work being done on the building). He had stood behind the CID men and brought the metal tube down between the two detectives! We now had two assaults.

The footballer was charged with assault and the original complainant was charged with causing grievous bodily harm with intent and the cases went to Crown Court. The prosecuting barrister came to me for a chat. The young visitor never contested the charge and was pleading guilty. Apparently, the young footballer on a lesser charge was contesting the case. It seemed the judge was content to just deal with the lad on the more serious charge who was pleading guilty. This meant the other lad would walk away! I was appalled, I told the prosecutor that if the footballer had not behaved as he did and assaulted the lad, the more serious offence would not have been committed. The prosecutor agreed to go back and talk to the judge and defence barrister. A compromise was reached and the young footballer pleaded guilty to a common law indictable assault occasioning actual bodily harm. The other lad received a non-custodial sentence. I often thought that lawyers must have been descendants of market traders. They were very good at doing deals.

I also had to investigate one of the serious fires on the Central Pier. I spent many hours investigating it, assisted by colleagues. No one was ever brought to court but I was convinced that the main female suspect who I interviewed on more than one occasion was responsible. However, there was insufficient evidence.

CHAPTER NINE
I'M NOW AN INSPECTOR

In December 1974, I was promoted to Section Inspector stationed at Blackpool Central. My colleague John Boyd was promoted on the same day. I was a uniform Inspector for about three years and I enjoyed this posting. It was an interesting post. On nights, you were responsible for the policing of all Blackpool and, of course, we had some busy nights. Early shift was an interesting one because after breakfast, we went to the prosecutions office and were given a number of cases to present and prosecute. Often, they were 'Not Guilty' cases and having only been given the file about 20 minutes before court commenced, you quickly learned to 'think on your feet'.

Young barristers sometimes appeared at the magistrate's court to gain experience. I once had to prosecute a 'Not Guilty' case and the defendant was represented by a young barrister. Good fortune was with me that day and I won. It did not always work out like that!

I once prosecuted a fortune-teller who allegedly gave personal readings. Two lady holidaymakers had been sat on the promenade and were chatting, it transpired that they had each gone to the same fortune teller for their personal reading and when they checked, they had got identical forecasts. I opened the case by stating that the fortune teller was clearly not proficient otherwise she should have been able to foretell her own misfortune. She gave me a withering look and I thought that I had better not milk this one otherwise I might be turned into a frog! However, the case was proved.

What I liked about this role was that although you had quite a lot of admin you were able to get out and supervise. Sometimes

I would use the car, but I also liked to walk. I would visit officers on their beats making sure they were doing what they were supposed to be doing and also checking that they were Ok.

Clearly, one cannot cover everything in a busy three years. One of my responsibilities when on duty was to visit licensed premises to ensure they were being run correctly. I would usually visit with a sergeant. I went round most of the public houses in my area. It was always interesting visiting at closing time. I went into one pub, 30 minutes after 'time called' and the place was heaving. Many people stood or were seated with full glasses. I approached the landlord and said, "Mr Landlord, have you an extension of your permitted hours"?

He replied "No", adding that it was very difficult to clear the premises.

I could have sympathised with his position but he was stood at the bar with customers and had a full pint in his hand. I gave him 'words of advice'.

I went round many pubs giving 'words of advice'. A friendly licensee told me that at a licensees' meeting, comment had been made about "The big black bastard with a stick" causing some sort of mayhem. I took that to be a reference to my black hair (no longer black) and the signalling stick which was an appointment.

I went into the Clifton Hotel basement bar one night. One got the feeling that trouble was imminent so I asked for the whereabouts of the manager and I was told that he was in the first floor cocktail bar with a couple of CID men. I went to the cocktail bar, and told him that he needed to come downstairs because trouble was very likely. It is not an exaggeration to say that he thought I was misreading the situation. However, we did go downstairs and there lying spread-eagled on the floor was one chap and a fight had occurred whilst we went for the manager. The manager was gracious enough to apologise.

I went into the ground floor bar of the same hotel on another occasion, again as I walked in, one sensed trouble. My suspicions were confirmed when the senior barman thanked us for coming in. There were two groups of men – one from Barrow in Furness and one from Wales. They were facing each other in a stand-off, but beckoning each other, obviously to a contest; clearly not a peaceful one. I spoke to the leader of the Welsh Group, well if he wasn't the leader he was certainly the mouthy one. I gave them 'words of advice' suggesting they leave in an orderly fashion.

'Mouthy' looked at me and sneeringly said words to the effect, "And will you be using that stick if we don't"?

I said "Yes," whereupon I signalled with my stick for the barman to pull down the shutters. The shutters duly came down and I told the group I was closing the bar for one hour. I have to say they were not for leaving. However, my Sergeant had called for back-up. Several cars arrived including the section van. All our lads waited outside and the section van driver, a man of some 6ft 4 inches plus, whose nickname was 'Roadblock' stood by the back doors of the van, ready to take custody of any miscreants. I pointed to my officers outside and told 'mouthy' that my team had arrived and the next move was down to him. Both groups left and dispersed, 'mouthy' telling me I would not last 'two minutes in the valleys'!

January 1975 started off well. Kathy passed her driving test! It was only her second attempt and she got the same driving examiner who failed her the first time. Apparently, he was quite nice.

Later in the year I was sent to Manchester on a Gaming Course. It was a five-day course. Our instructor was the Gaming Board Inspector who used to be responsible for the Westminster area in London where serious gambling took place. We visited Casinos in the Manchester city centre and Bingo Halls. It was an interesting course, but the problem was that in the Police Service, when you went on a specialised course you were regarded as the expert.

On my return to division, I was asked to write a piece for the local newspaper about lotteries etc. I submitted my paper to the Chief Inspector and said that I would appreciate him casting his eye over it to see if it was sound. He looked at me, signed it off and said, "I'll sink or swim with you"!

Margaret Thatcher became leader of the Conservative opposition in 1975 and that October attended her first party conference as leader. I was the duty Inspector at the Winter Gardens and one of her chief aides came to me and said as it was her first conference it would be nice if there was a crowd when she came out at lunchtime. I assured him there would be and he seemed surprised that I said this. I was not favouring his party leader, what he did not know at that time, is that at all the conferences we always put the crowd barriers up at lunchtime and when the conference was finishing. Now once you put the barriers out, they would always attract a crowd and they did. Mrs Thatcher came out to meet and greet and even signed the foot of a young person's Gonk Toy!

At the end of the Conference some of us were invited to the Imperial Hotel to meet Mrs Thatcher for a drink. Whilst in the queue, one of the Tory faithful sarcastically said words to the effect, "The Police will always be first in line for a free drink".

He was speedily put in his place by the booming voice of Willy Whitelaw who said, "But they are always beaten by the likes of us"!

Just to balance it up, during the premiership of James Callaghan which was between 5th April 1976 and 4 May 1979, I was with a group at the Imperial Hotel. Mr Callaghan and his wife had separated and were each going round the group chatting, when he came to me we chatted generally about family and I mentioned that our son Darren was in a pop group. He turned and called his wife over and told her about Darren being in a pop group. We had quite a nice chat and I got the impression that he found it refreshing to talk about such things.

1976 for me was an interesting year because I attended an Inspectors' pre-college course at Hutton from 19 January until 20 February. On 29 March I attended the Inspectors' Course at the Home Office National Training Establishment at Bramshill House in Hampshire. That course had approximately 140 Inspectors attending and we were split into syndicates. It was a full and demanding course and I used to travel home every other weekend. Kathy brought Darren to Bramshill for a weekend, Bramshill House was set in acres of grounds and had a boating lake. Dennis, a friend took Darren sailing and Darren's assessment of Bramshill was "It's like a gentlemen's club". And that was the view of a 13-year-old!

I really enjoyed my time at Bramshill; I enjoyed the time and chance to research – they had a fabulous library. Each Inspector had to submit an essay for a book prize. I did not win the book prize, but I came in the first three. The course finished on 11 June and I was glad to get back to my operational duties.

During the summer, I set up a plain clothes team of young officers to enter mock auction sales with a view to obtaining evidence of wrong doing. They would dress as holiday makers and would record the sales pitch. This proved a cumbersome and time consuming practice. The Mock Auction Act 1961 defined a Mock Auction as:

Subject to the following provisions of this section, for the purposes of this Act a sale of goods by way of competitive bidding shall be taken to be a mock auction if, but only if, during the course of the sale– (a) any lot to which this Act applies is sold to a person bidding for it, and either it is sold to him at a price lower than the amount of his highest bid for that lot, or part of the price at which it is sold to him is repaid or credited to him or is stated to be so repaid or credited, or (b) the right to bid for any lot to which this Act applies is restricted, or is stated to be restricted, to persons who have bought or agreed to buy one or more articles, or (c) any articles are given away or offered as gifts.

A sale of goods shall not be taken to be a mock auction by virtue of paragraph (a) of the last preceding subsection, if it is proved that the reduction in price, or the repayment or credit, as the case may be,– (a) was on account of a defect discovered after the highest bid in question had been made, being a defect of which the person conducting the sale was unaware when that bid was made, or (b) was on account of damage sustained after that bid was made.

It was without doubt a complex piece of legislation open to interpretation which of course, meant solicitors got the chance to earn! We received many complaints about the activities of the Mock Auction team; people turning up at the Police Station distressed having lost much money.

I trained the officers so they had a good grasp of the legislation and had the confidence to stop the sale, at a point where they felt there was sufficient evidence to prove a case. Hitherto, by the time we had transcribed the lengthy tape recordings; some of the salesmen were difficult to trace to report them for summons. Now there were shorter recordings and the salesmen could be identified and reported at the time.

We could never put the owner in the premises when the offences were being committed. However, one day he was in a saleroom when the team stopped the sale and he had been present when the offending activity had taken place. When the officers stopped the sale, he tried to intervene. One officer said, "What's it got to do with you".

He replied that he was the owner and it was his saleroom. (They were fateful words because at Crown Court in December 1976, he received a suspended prison sentence. It did not stop the auctions but we did not see much of him at the premises).

On 30 August that year, I was on nights and had only been in bed for about an hour when I was awakened with the news,

"Sam, the Guinea Pig is dead". Sam was named after a police dog. I raised my weary body and went to the bottom of the garden to dig a grave. The ground was rock hard. But Sam was put in an old shoe box and buried and a tree log placed on top with his name inscribed thereon. What you do for your son!

1977 did not start too well for me. I was on night duty on Friday 18 February and during the night I was suffering from what I thought was indigestion. I managed to get a 'bottle' from the A & E department and was 'swigging' away at this. We got a call in the late evening/early hours of trouble at the Norbreck Hotel. When I arrived, there were people running about, some chasing others. It was like a scene from the Keystone Cops. We had to grip the situation and the team did.

It transpired that a lad had been causing trouble and had been quite properly ejected from the hotel bar. However, once he was outside the bouncers set about him and injured him. Witnesses were outside and told us that there was absolutely no reason for the bouncers to act in the manner they did and it was not just one witness but several. The offenders were identified and arrested. The manager came out and said that if we arrested all his security men, aka bouncers, he would have to close the bar. I told him that is what he must do.

I finished duty at 7am. The Inspector taking over said I did not look too good. Prior to going to work that night, I had eaten home cooked chips. Being a typical man, I blamed Kathy saying the chips were probably undercooked. Her reply was that I had eaten them too quickly! I went to bed but found it difficult to breathe and experienced some pain and discomfort so I went to my surgery and saw Dr Lucking who ran a Saturday morning clinic. After examining me he sent me to Victoria Hospital where I remained until 3 March.

I was initially diagnosed by the Consultant Physician as suffering from an embolism. That changed when I mentioned that a few days before, I had been giving blood when there was a blockage and the doctor had to attend to the cannula, after that, the diagnosis became 'a virus'. I was readmitted for three days in April and the Consultant Surgeon could not understand why I had been taken off the blood thinning injections.

I was very well looked after in hospital. On one occasion, my mother visited with Kathy and Darren and started to tell us about all the relatives who died. Darren was 14 years old at the time and he and I cracked up laughing, which actually affected my health and the next day, there was a notice on the room door stating, "Family Visitors Only"! That was odd as it was my mother who unintentionally caused the problem.

My condition was finally diagnosed as a 'Pleural Effusion' which means that there is a build-up of fluid between a lung and the chest wall. During my first stay, a young doctor who I suspect was learning the new procedure drained the fluid or attempted to! It was a painful procedure and I could feel the needle going in.

The Divisional Chief Superintendent visited me at home and I think he had been trained by my mother, he was telling Kathy and me how many Inspectors had recently died. He was a cheerful soul!

Licensing was a complicated subject. One of the things licensees had to be fully aware of was that they had a vicarious responsibility. One nightclub owner fell afoul of this, it was the well-respected former heavyweight boxer Brian London. Brian generally ran his clubs well. On 10 July 1977, in the late evening I was walking along Bank Hey Street with Sergeant Keith Sinclair when we were approached by a group of lads who wanted to know where the 007 club was. I told them that it was round the corner, pointing to Victoria Street but advising them that they would be wasting their time as they had to be members. The lad winked at me. I started to continue walking towards Talbot Square then stopped.

I said to the sergeant "We just have to check this out".

We went to the club and on entering, the man supposed to be controlling entry sat behind a high desk with his feet on the desk. The sergeant and I were in uniform which made not the slightest difference to the guy who was admitting other people. I told Sergeant Sinclair to go upstairs and to check two people at random to ascertain if they were members. He brought down two people, neither of whom were members.

The normal procedure would be to submit a report, which apparently went to Force HQ who would decide if observations should be kept etc., with a view to some action being taken. I took the view that immediate action was required and I called for all available patrols to be sent to the club and sufficient officers responded for us to take action. Over 60 people were in the club at the time of our visit, the majority of who were not members and more than a dozen who were unaccounted for hurriedly left the premises by the rear fire escape.

It transpired that Brian London was on holiday at the time of our visit. On 6 February 1978, he faced sanctions by the justices. As he left court, he said, "Is it personal Mr Meadows"?

I assured him it was not. In truth he had been very badly let down by those he left in charge which I thought was a great shame because he was a decent nightclub owner.

In August 1977, we took a holiday in Cornwall and when we saw the many adverts for 'clotted cream teas' it certainly reminded me of my hospital experience.

In September the TUC Congress was held at the Winter Gardens, Blackpool. In those days we only needed about dozen police officers to police it but this week was going to be so different. The first challenge was that a member or members of the Shrewsbury Pickets was believed to be coming. I was told by the TUC organisers that in the unlikely event of trouble, we may be asked to enter the Congress Hall. This could be a problem,

I explained to them that I was not going to enter the hall, simply on a request. Imagine the fallout if it was a false call. They had to identify a steward who would come to me direct with the request. They agreed to this and one of General Secretary Len Murray's aides brought a bearded chap to me and said if he requested the police to enter, it would be a genuine request.

As it turned out, there was no trouble, just a flurry of TV cameras etc., when the Shrewsbury Pickets' team arrived.

However, the challenges were to increase. The Right to Work Campaign were marching to Blackpool. Several Police Support Units (PSU's) had been brought in but were kept at Divisional Headquarters. As stated earlier, I was deployed with approximately a dozen officers. Barriers had been erected and several groups were situated behind the barriers to make peaceful protests. As it got busier I radioed in and suggested that more officers should be sent. Many PSU's had been brought in anticipating that there may be problems. I was told that another PSU (usually one inspector three sergeants and 18 constables) would attend the Winter Gardens. I suggested that as another Inspector was being deployed, a more senior officer should take over command. Superintendent John Brown came out and said that he would be the commanding officer but as I had an understanding of the situation, he said that I should advise how men should be deployed.

The march arrived approaching along Church Street from the east. I spoke to the members of the group. I told them that two or three of their leaders could go to the front but the rest must go behind the other protesters who had been in situ for a long time. It would have been very unfair to them to let all the marchers go in front. My words were totally ignored. Their arrival had coincided with the lunch break for the Congress delegates. The marchers totally ignored my instructions and charged towards the delegates. There was a white Bedford Van accompanying the marchers and I approached a man who appeared to be a leader and I asked him to help me restore order by addressing his marchers. He refused.

We had to protect the delegates and the marchers then headed off to the beach for a meeting. It was clear that they intended coming back so we decided to put a phalanx of officer across Church Street/Abingdon Street to block them off.

Eventually the 'Right to Work' marchers returned. Our officers had been told to prevent any marchers getting through. However, the white Bedford Van was leading and came up to the line of police officers. The man I had spoken to earlier was by the driver's open door. This man I learned to be John Deason. He had a megaphone and I heard him shout to the driver, "Drive through". The van did and drove through the officers' line. I had to tell one officer who was at the front of the van to let go otherwise he would have been hurt. The van drove on and stopped and I went up to it. Deason was still with it and I told him he was being arrested. I took him to the front of the Winter Gardens and as I did, the TUC stewards lined up as if to block my path. I told them to move which they did and I took Deason to a small office and left him with a sergeant.

As soon as Deason was arrested, many of the marchers put on badges which said, "Free John Deason". They all then went down to Divisional HQ and surrounded the complex.

Blackpool Division had an excellent prosecution solicitor Mr Arnold Brewer. I used to ask Mr Brewer to get Richard Henriques to act for us if he was free. It was good to get him on 'the side of the Angels'.

At Deason's trial which took place between 27 and 2 March 1978 at Preston Crown Court, Mr Henriques appeared for the crown and Deason was defended by Mr John Melville Williams QC. After a three-day trial, Deason was found guilty by a majority verdict of 'Inciting an unknown person to drive a transit van recklessly by driving it through a police cordon during a demonstration outside the Winter Gardens, Blackpool, where the TUC Conference was taking place'. He was also found guilty of threatening behaviour likely to cause a breach of the peace but not guilty of assaulting PC Willie Peacock and PC Tom Kettlewell who were struck by the van but not injured. Deason had denied all the charges and was given a six month prison sentence suspended for two years by Judge Keith Dewhurst.

Richard Henriques later successfully prosecuted the two ten-year-old boys, Robert Thompson and Jon Venables who murdered three-year-old James Patrick Bulger. He later became Mr Justice Henriques and since he retired has undertaken some high profile enquiries.

On 5 October 1977, Inspector Les James from Lancaster Division and I attend a pre-briefing at The Hough End Centre, Greater Manchester Police's Sports and Social Centre. Martin Webster the National Front Leader was to march through Hyde, a full march having been banned. A full scale police operation was being mounted and mutual aid from neighbouring force would be required. Over 2,000 police officers would be deployed. We were served airline type meals and were told that this is what the troops would get on the day.

When 9 October arrived Les James and I each took a PSU. We had set off early and our first stop was at a school for breakfast. The bacon served resulted in several comments of "insist on the real thing Formica" a popular TV advert at the time. However the advert was for a laminate produced for kitchen worktops etc., not for bacon! Then we went to the centre of Hyde and were based in a school. My good friend Sergeant Mike Woodruff finished up sitting in a Wendy type house!

We were told to wait until we were called for lunch. The lunch turned out to be soup, served in plastic beakers and a sandwich. However, when I saw an opportunity, I got my lads fed and Les did the same, much to the annoyance of a Chief Inspector who was the catering officer. He told us that we were an undisciplined lot. It was just as well we did eat then because circumstances meant that we were turned out and would not have had the time to eat.

We bought fish and chips on the way home. I submitted a report when I returned to Lancashire to ensure none of the officers was out of pocket having had to purchase a meal.

On 21 November 1977, I received a telephone call from Acting Deputy Chief Constable Ronald Rowbottom. He told me that they had been looking at promotions and transfers. He said I was not being considered for a promotion, but for a transfer to the Regional Crime Squad. He told me to think about it and let him know.

That afternoon I popped into Divisional HQ and went to see the sub-divisional superintendent Harold Cawley. Roy Lenton, the second in command of the division was chatting to him, these were two people I had the greatest respect for and I told them of the call from Force Headquarters. Roy Lenton was bemused because no one had been in touch with Divisional Command. Harold said it would be 'another string to your bow' and Roy said that I should never turn down offers. When I got home I called Mr Rowbottom and said I would be happy to move and on 5 December, I transferred to the No 1 Regional Crime Squad (RCS).

I had to think seriously about whether I wanted to go on the RCS. Unlike the National Crime Agency of today it did not operate as I felt it should. The dreaded targets were in play and the squad would often deal with cases that should really have been left to the local CID.

I had to go to Manchester to see the No 1 RCS Commander, a Detective Chief Superintendent. Generally we had a pleasant interview and it was Jeff this and Jeff that, until he said that as a uniform Inspector I must be thrilled to be joining the RCS. I said that I had thought carefully about it because I was reasonably well thought of as a section Inspector and I wasn't sure about joining a 'stagnant outfit'! That shook him up a bit and he said, "Well, at least you are honest Mr Meadows".

I did try to give the Blackpool Branch Squad some better direction and let them investigate crime which was more fitting to a regional group. There were some very good detectives in the branch who had a lot of experience.

I was once on surveillance in the Manchester area keeping tabs on a suspect vehicle. Lo and behold the Fire Engine turned up to 'a car on fire' report, it being the one under surveillance! Clearly, we had been clocked.

I did go on a surveillance course and we trained in busy areas, such as Liverpool, Blackpool and even travelled down to Wales. We were trained on foot and vehicle surveillance. I also attended a Hostage Negotiator's Course run by the Metropolitan Police. It was a fascinating course but I was never used because shortly after, I got promoted to DCI and the view at that time was that the ideal rank for a negotiator was Inspector.

As RCS officers could be armed, I decided to go on a firearm course and Lancashire Constabulary was one of the National Firearm Training Centres. On one occasion we had to be tested at the Army's Close Quarter Battle Range at Holcombe Moor, Bury. There were about a dozen of us and as I was the only ranking officer, I was volunteered and agreed to go first. That was a mistake. I set off with a loaded .38 revolver through long grass and trees when all of a sudden a target, previously lying flat in the long grass, sprung up in front of me. To say it was a shock is an understatement and I went down on one knee and fired away, missing the target. I must have thought I was John Wayne. There was a tap on my shoulder and Sergeant Blackburn the firearms instructor yelled, "Who the fucking hell taught you to shoot like that Sir. Not me Sir"! Anyway I did pass the course. I knew why I had been volunteered to go first, the lads and lasses timed from when I set off to my first shot so they had an idea when the first target would appear!

On one occasion whilst on RCS I had to give evidence at a Crown Court appeal, which related to the time when I was a uniform Inspector. A local nightclub owner was appealing against a decision by the justices to remove his licence. Richard Henriques was appearing for the Crown. Several section Inspectors were called to give evidence. There had been a lot of trouble at this particular club which seemed to attract some punk rockers.

One of my colleagues was asked by the Judge what was so different about Punk Rockers. The Inspector answered that they wore safety pins. The Judge remarked that he wore safety pins in his cardigan but he wasn't a punk rocker. Sadly, the Inspector did not tell the Judge that he may wear safety pins in his clothing but not through his nose!

Judge William Openshaw, affectionately known as Granite Bill was presiding. One of the points being made by the appellant's counsel was that other clubs which had breached the law had not received the same sanction as him. I had some knowledge of the reason and said I could assist the Court. The appellant's lawyer jumped at the chance thinking I would assist his client. Things did not go too well. After I answered a question from the appellant's lawyer, Judge Openshaw spoke to me and said, "When you leave this court, take a look in a mirror and you will see that you are wearing a suit of clothes, not a wig and gown". He was reminding me that I was not presenting the case.

I replied, "With the greatest of respect Your Honour, I am trying to answer a question from the appellant's counsel", to which the Judge quickly responded with the comment, "If you are asked an unintelligible question, don't give an unintelligible answer".

I still had not the made the important point I wanted to make, so I thought 'in for a penny – in for a pound'. I started to try and get the point in but was quickly ordered out of the witness box and despatched by the Judge.

After the lunch break, Richard Henriques light heartedly said to me that Tony Hammond had finished in court so I could borrow his wig and gown and go back in court. I declined that offer knowing full well that the Judge had the power to send me to the cells for contempt!

As it turned out, I was only in the RCS for seven months before being promoted to Detective Chief Inspector (DCI) by Acting Chief Constable John Moody. I did receive a nice comment from Detective Chief Superintendent Bill Lumsden the Number One RCS Commander who wished me well and said, "You have breathed new life into the Blackpool Branch".

A good support to me when I was Uniform Inspector was Mike Woodruff. Mike was one of the best sergeants I have worked with. He nurtured his constables and looked after them very well. He in turn was very well respected. Mike had a great sense of humour, I was once typing out a report about resources and I was paraphrasing Sir Winston's famous quote, "Give us the tools, and we will finish the job".

Mike read the report and said, "Well they have given us the tools, and what a load of tools they are"!

I had a lot of time for Mike and his good friend, retired sergeant Alan Barnes. Alan had cancer and died on 28 October 2015. Mike and I visited him a few days before he died. It is always sad to lose a colleague and friend and we seem to lose too many. Mike lost his wife Cynthia, and years later he lost a loving Partner Jean. I am pleased to say that he has found contentment with a wonderful lady Rita.

What I also learned was that the advice I had received from Chief Superintendent Roy Lenton, one should never turn down a job offer was so apposite. If I had turned down the offer to go on the RCS, would I have been promoted to Detective Chief Inspector?

CHAPTER TEN
PROMOTION TO DETECTIVE CHIEF INSPECTOR

On 1 July 1978, I started as Deputy Head of the Number One District Task Force (later to become the Area Crime Squad). The squad would be called in to assist Divisional personnel whenever there was a murder or serious crime. As Deputy, I also had a responsibility for the uniformed crime patrol officers and dog handlers.

At one Labour Party Conference, the Task force had responsibility for security at the Imperial Hotel. The CID officers were on internal duties and the uniformed members of the team secured the entrances and patrolled the external grounds.

Every morning a bus left the hotel to take the platform party to the Winter Gardens. A very senior member of the Party missed the bus and saw it disappearing on the Promenade. He turned to the uniformed sergeant, a former RAF veteran and asked if there was any way the bus could be slowed down, whereupon the sergeant responded, "Yes Sir, nationalise it". On another day, and arrogant delegate shouted to a constable, "Officer, call me a taxi".

Yes, you have guessed it, the constable replied, "Very Good Sir, you're a taxi".

Interestingly, I received no complaint from either delegate!

It was a great job which I had until promotion to Superintendent in March 1982.

There were many interesting cases we had to deal with. When a murder or other serious crime took place, a control room was set up with different squads operating. I usually took charge of the 'Follow-up Squad', which meant I had to prioritise enquiries as they came in and allocate them to my team.

THE MURDER OF ALAN LIVESEY

(Details of this case can be found in *'Murder in Lancashire – Notorious Cases and How They Were Solved'* by Ian Hunter, ISBN: 9-78-1-874181-91-0.)

On 22 February 1979, a murder took place in Bamber Bridge. A 14-year-old Army Cadet Alan Livesey was stabbed to death and bound. His mother Margaret Livesey was subsequently convicted of murdering Alan. There were two trials and she was found guilty in July 1979 and sentenced to life imprisonment. She did retract her confession and her case was featured on the BBC's *Rough Justice* series. A re-investigation in 1983 by West Yorkshire Police and the Court of Appeal in 1986 came to the conclusion that the verdict was correct.

Margaret Livesey was released from prison in 1989 on life parole but in November 2001 died of throat cancer.

I was not involved in any of the interviews but in the early part of the original investigation I had the job of visiting local schools and the army cadets seeking information, accompanied by the media.

THE MURDER OF MAUD HOGAN

(Details of this case can be found in *'Murder in Lancashire – Notorious Cases and How They Were Solved'* by Ian Hunter, ISBN: 9-78-1-874181-91-0.)

On 17 March 1979 following the murder of 89-year-old Maud Hogan who lived in Lancaster, the murder team supported local detectives investigating her death. She had died in her bed with injuries to her head. In his book *Murder in Lancashire* Ian Hunter, the Detective Superintendent, then second in command of

Lancashire CID commented on the fact that two spent matches and a button were found in the deceased's living room. It transpired that the pathologists had lit his pipe in that room and the button came from the jacket of a Detective Sergeant who visited the scene.

I headed up the 'Follow-Up' Squad. Two local youths were arrested and convicted of her untimely death. I well remember that the button was thought to be very important until a very embarrassed Detective Sergeant disclosed it was from his jacket.

THE MURDER OF MARTIN CHRISTOPHER JOHNSTONE

(Details of this case can be found in *'Greed The Mr Asia Connection'* by Richard Hall, ISBN: 0 330 27015X, which can still be found on Amazon and in *'Murder in Lancashire – Notorious Cases and How They Were Solved'* by Ian Hunter, ISBN: 978-1-874181-91-0.)

In October 1979 amateur divers came across a body in Eccleston Delph, near Chorley. The hands had been removed and the body weighted down with weights. So began my involvement with what became known as the 'Handless Corpse' case or the 'Mr Asia' case.

This was a dream case for a detective. As usual, I took charge of the 'Follow-Up' Squad based in Chorley Divisional Headquarters. For two weeks we could not identify the body until the girlfriend of the deceased and a female who turned out to be the girlfriend of one of the assassins walked into a police station to say they knew who the murdered man was.

Detective Superintendent Ray Rimmer was the senior investigating officer. He was a great detective and first class leader. He was supported by Detective Superintendent Phil Cafferky. This was a case of a drug dealer, executed on the orders of the syndicate boss – a killing that sparked off an international murder investigation.

According to a report in Hansard on 10 March 1982, the cost of the 'handless corpse' trial was estimated at £1.3 million, but the total estimate, which included security measures and courtroom alterations, plus the expected appeals was £2,178,450. Sir Patrick Mayhew, the Home Office Minister at that time said the trial proved to be the most expensive hearing on record and (it) was almost the longest for a murder case. He went onto say, "The investigation was a great credit to the force and to the people who sustained that force…"

During the debate, the boss of the drug syndicate, Alexander James Sinclaire, also known as Terry Clark, was said to have, "…amassed a fortune estimated at £25 million from drug racketeering within the space of four years."

Sir Patrick talked of the fears expressed as to what might have happened if witnesses talked to the police. He told Members of Parliament, "High security had to be provided throughout that period within the precincts of the court and for the trial judge, Mrs Justice Heilbron, and, as I have mentioned, for witnesses. Without that high level of security it is probable that attempts would have been made either on the lives of witnesses or to effect the release of some of the accused from the court."

I give a presentation about this case and sometimes refer to it *as 'a glimpse into murder investigation'*. Why? – Because my presentation primarily deals with my involvement. In the main, murder investigation is about teamwork and hard slog! – With a touch of luck. All too often, we see television detectives solving crimes on their own – that is not true life, well at least in the United Kingdom.

The murdered man was Martin Christopher Johnstone who at the time of the murder in 1979 was 27 years of age. Sometime in the mid 1970's, Johnstone moved from New Zealand to Australia where he apparently teamed up with Andrew Samuel Maher who in 1979 was 26 years of age and Alexander James Sinclaire, who was 35 years. When they met up, Sinclaire was using the name Terry Clark. Clark is said to have used some 33 names and used several disguises

With others, the three men formed a drug smuggling syndicate, mainly involved in the smuggling of drugs from Thailand into Australasia. At the height of its operation, the syndicate used many vessels to transport large quantities of drugs from Thailand to Australasia. They had an ocean going yacht called *'The Brigadoon'*, which Johnstone had purchased. Mechanical problems were experienced with that boat and it was replaced with a larger fishing vessel called *'The Kompira'*.

They also set up several companies in Australia, Hong Kong and Singapore from the proceeds of illegal drugs. It is worth noting at this point, that several persons connected with the ring who had given information to the police were found murdered in Australia. Great problems were caused for the syndicate as a result of the police enquiries which followed those murders – Sinclaire and Maher moved to England, their intention to set up a drug smuggling ring in this country.

Johnstone enjoyed the good life, however, their drug smuggling activities attracted massive publicity in Australia and the Far East putting pressure on the syndicate and things began to fall apart.

Clark had started to deal direct, cutting Johnstone out of the deals. He also switched from Thai Sticks to heroin. This meant the drug couriers could use aircraft. Johnstone, who had bought at least two more confiscated trawlers from the Australian Government, was left with idle ships and a disgruntled crew.

Relations had become strained between Johnstone and Sinclaire, but in May 1979, at a meeting in Singapore, a so called 'reconciliation' took place. Following that meeting Johnstone and Maher subsequently flew to England to see Clark. Johnstone was given $A50, 000 by Clark to find a new source of heroin. When

Johnstone returned to Singapore he put the $A50, 000 into a safe deposit box owned by Monique Van Putten. Then on 1 August 1979, they went to Pattaya in Thailand a place known to many tourists..

    Johnstone had changed $A35,000 into Thai notes. They were there to do a deal for heroin at a house at Chonburi, a town about ten miles from Pattaya. They met three armed Thai dealers and Johnstone was shown 700 grammes of pure heroin in a plastic bag. He tested it and being satisfied, sent Monique back to the hotel for the money, much against her will. The Thais took Monique back to the hotel for the money and she feared for her life.

    Johnstone got back to the hotel at 4am. He had fallen for the old trick. The Thais had shown him some packages, took the money from him on the pretext of counting it, and then the van sped away. He had been left with that one sample bag. What did not help is that one of Clark's henchmen was waiting in Singapore to take the heroin back to England.

    Johnstone and Maher stayed in a Bangkok for a couple of days, then desperate, Johnstone took the 700-gramme sample bag and cut it with castor sugar. In doing so, Johnstone had signed his own death warrant. When Clark found out what happened, he was not a happy man. Johnstone had to be disposed of, and it was decided to entice him back to England, on the pretence of a fictitious drug deal. Andy Maher was given the task.

    He had recruited his 'cousin' James Smith (actually his father's stepbrother) as a courier. Smith encountered problems getting visas for him and other couriers. It was then that Maher persuaded Smith to help him in what was to be the execution of Martin Christopher Johnstone.

    The plan was they could put Johnstone in touch with a man in Glasgow, who could supply drug couriers and put up £40,000. Maher told Smith that he was the only person who could be trusted. He convinced Smith that it was because of the safety of his (Maher's) partner, Barbara Pilkington and their daughter, he had to do it.

Of the conversation, Smith was later to say, "He (Maher) was getting excited and upset. He said that the people involved had killed people before. He said they wouldn't think twice."

Smith agreed to help 'to sell Martin the dummy story about the couriers'. Maher said he would need some help to dispose of the body. Smith agreed but said he would not kill Johnstone. The plan was put into operation and Johnstone arrived in England accompanied by his girlfriend Julie Hue. Smith also collected the gun from a courier at Preston Railway Station. She had travelled by train from London.

Johnstone spent a couple of days in London and then travelled to Leyland in Lancashire. On Tuesday 9 October 1979, he left Leyland to go to Glasgow for the supposed drug deal. He was never seen alive again!

On Sunday, 14 October 1979, amateur sub-aqua divers were practising in Eccleston Quarry where the waters go to a depth of 100 feet when they came across a mutilated body.

Police USU divers attended the scene. PC Arthur Marshall helped to pull the body into the boat.

It was found that attempts had been made to disfigure the face and the hands had been hacked off and were missing. Tied to the body were a number of 14 lb. weights, 56 lb. weights, and to make sure it stayed down a heavy duty motor vehicle jack.

A post mortem examination by Dr Garrett, revealed that death had been caused by a bullet wounds to the head. One .38 calibre bullet was subsequently recovered from the head. There were stab wounds to the stomach, but these had apparently been caused after death. The hands had also been removed after death.

The police were called. As mentioned earlier, the enquiry was led by the late Detective Superintendent (later to become Det Chief Supt) Ray Rimmer. To use a Lancashire expression, Ray was a gradely Blackburn lad – whose unique leadership style led to a successful conclusion of the case.

Well, the investigation commenced and a full team was assembled for the next morning. Each Detective Chief Inspector was given his own area of responsibility. I was in charge of the 'follow-up' squad. There was a weight squad, House to House enquiry squad, location and movement squad to check car sightings, medallion squad to trace the origins of a medallion found round the deceased's neck, forensic team, licensed house squad, dentist squad, to name but a few. We had no idea who the deceased was at that time. A photograph of the dead man was widely circulated. For over two weeks we tried, without success to identify the deceased.

Tuesday, 30 October 1979 was a significant date because Barbara Pilkington and Julie Hue came forward and told the police who the murdered man was. The game was up.

I was given the job of taking charge of all enquires in Scotland. This meant I was to interview James Smith one of the two assassins.

When you are involved in a murder enquiry, events can dictate the pace, and after a briefing from Ray and his colleague, I was on my way to Scotland with two Detective Sergeants and two Detective Constables. I remember very clearly; we arrived at the home of James Smith in Livingston at 5.30pm that Tuesday evening. He agreed to go with us to Livingston Police Station. We had two interviews with him that night and it was clear he was a worried man. However, he denied being involved in any murder, he agreed he knew Martin Johnstone and said Maher and Johnstone had dropped him off before they went onto to Glasgow. We put it to him he was involved and he denied it.

Obviously, the interviews we had with Smith and later Maher formed a major part of the evidence against them. All the interviews, I mention were given in open court which is why I can use them.

The next morning again with Det Sgt Wright and DC Fleming, we saw Smith in the cells at Bathgate Police Station. He persisted in his denials.

I then spoke to him and said, "You say you are innocent?"

Smith replied, "Aye".

I asked, "How far are you prepared to go to prove that innocence?"

Smith replied, "All the way".

I said, "Even to the extent of returning with me to Chorley?"

Smith replied, "Aye".

So off we went to the murder headquarters at Chorley Police Station. We left Bathgate at 2.30pm arriving at Chorley at 5.45pm. At 7.40pm that day we started to interview Smith again. We put it to him that he had killed Johnstone.

He continued with his denials but began to tremble – and later he admitted he was frightened for his family, we tried to reassure him. There were many long pauses and then he admitted that he was present saying, "Aye, but I never killed him; I nearly fucking died myself with shock." And then the truth was out. In an hour-long interview he told us the whole gory tale.

Richard Hall very kindly wrote in his book *'Greed'*; "The interrogation by Detective Chief Inspector Meadows and Detective Constable Fleming is something of a classic of its kind". I'm not going to argue with that! Interestingly, he described me as 'something of a thinking policeman' and he was correct to say that I 'would hate that phrase'. It can suggest that thinking policemen are a rare breed, but what he did also was to refer to a frame extract from the Criminal Law Review in 1960, which I had displayed in my office.

> *The nervous pressure of guilt is enormous; the load of the deed done is heavy; the fear of detection fills the consciousness; and when the detection comes, the pressure is relieved; and the deep sense of relief makes confession a satisfaction. At that moment, he will tell all, and tell it truly. To forbid soliciting him, to seek to prevent this relief, is to fly in the face of human nature. It is natural and should be lawful, to take his confession at that moment – the best one. And this expedient, if sanctioned, saves the state a delay and expense in convicting him after he has reacted from his first sensations, has yielded to his friends solicitations, and comes under the sway of the natural human instinct to struggle to save himself by the aid of all technicalities.*
>
> *Lord Justice Wigmore*
Criminal Law Review 1960
Pages 334-335

I think that Lord Justice Wigmore's quote was very interesting and James Smith certainly seemed relieved to confess. I invited Smith to make a written statement – known as a voluntary statement. It commenced at 8.40pm and terminated at 5.10am the next morning.

This is James Smith's account of the murder as dictated to me:

We set off about twenty to ten the Tuesday night. We went in Andrew's brown Jaguar. Martin wanted to drive first but that would have upset Andrew's plan so he insisted on driving… We went on the A6 road because Andrew didn't want to go on the motorway because of the heavies. When we got to Lancaster we got a bit confused with the one-way system and we stopped by the taxi rank at the bus station. Andrew asked a taxi driver how to get onto the A6... and the taxi driver directed us... after we had gone on for a while, perhaps 20 minutes, Andrew stopped the car. He said to Martin, who had been sat in the front passenger seat, "Hey, I thought you wanted to drive". Martin said, "Alright". Martin opened the passenger car door... and was actually in the car... Andrew had concealed the gun under his jacket, He took the gun, leaned over and placed the gun very close to Martin's head and shot him at close range in the head... The noise was deafening. I felt stunned. I hadn't expected Andrew to do it so quick because he didn't want to be back at the house before 1am and I expected it to be done in Scotland. When he was shot, Martin sort of jerked and fell onto the ground outside the car. He sort of fell in a heap. Andrew jumped out and he shouted to me. I was in the back of the car. I got out. Martin was making a sound. It wasn't a moan as such. It was a horrible sound, more like a gurgle. Andrew was stood... close to Martin. He was bending over and he pointed the gun... Andrew shot Martin again. This time he shot him at the side of his head near to his temple. I think it was the right side. We put Martin back into the front passenger seat and dropped the back of the seat so that it was lying back. I could still hear the gurgling sounds as though he was trying to breathe and even then he was sort of jerking. We were both panicking a bit by this time. Andrew got into the driving seat. I had to get into the offside passenger seat – that's when Andrew started to try and start the car – Martin was still gurgling and Andrew turned round and said, "For fucks sake can't you stop that noise?" I said, "Andrew, the guy's dead." He said, "Fucking stab him or something." I said, "For fucks sake, he's dead".

They made their way back south and in the vicinity of Ingol, near Preston they decided to put Johnstone's body into the boot of the Jaguar. When they had done this they drove round for a while then made their way back to Maher's house in Robin Hey, Leyland. His house garage was not attached to the house, but was at the rear.

The house lights were on, so they dumped the body in the garage and then went to Southport and also checked the quarry to make sure that there would be no problems. Interestingly enough, Smith, Maher and a friend Billy Kirby had been to the quarry the previous night to check it out.

Now Billy was quite a lad. He'd been employed by Johnstone and had a nice line in making false bottoms for suitcases. However, on this particular occasion he had provided Maher with some weights, a hatchet, the hammer, rope, polythene sheet and a car jack.

They arrived back at the garage at about 1.30am to 2am. We'll let James Smith take up the story again, bearing in mind that they had discussed ways of preventing the identification of the body:

> We changed into overalls... Andrew said, "Come on, let's strip him." I took shoes and trousers off. In fact I took all the clothing off because Andrew was taking rings off his fingers. Andrew kept one particular ring. It had a blue stone, a large ring. He told me he was keeping it to show someone that he had knocked off Martin. It was some sort of proof. All Andrew said was, "it's for that guy down there." Martin was lying on his back with his head towards the garage door... Andrew picked an axe up and started to chops the hands from Martin's body. I turned away but it didn't take him very long to do it. While he was chopping his hands off he asked me to smash Martin's teeth. I picked up a lump hammer. I rested it on his face to steady my aim but I couldn't lift it up and go through with it. I felt sick. I told him I was sorry and I couldn't do it. He said, "Well put

something on his fucking face and do it." He finished chopping his hands off and put them in a brown paper bag, more like a big envelope. He told me to tie a small weight onto the bag with the hands in, whilst he did the teeth. He covered Martin's face with my blue and white jumper and he hit the face, about twice, with the hammer then threw it down. I think he was just about cracking up. We got hold of some wire mesh to wrap round the body so we could attach the weights. Just then a car pulled up outside the garage. At that point the two of us were not worth a fuck and that car coming up destroyed us. The car stayed a couple of minutes and drove off. That was me finished. I didn't bother with the mesh and we tied the weights onto the body with some blue nylon rope... I forgot to mention... Andrew tried to cut Martin's stomach. He said that he'd heard that bodies which had been weighted down with concrete had come up because the body had bloated. He said, "We'll have to cut his stomach open." He felt it would keep him down. He took hold of a shovel; well it was more a garden spade. He hit the body with the spade but the spade bounced off. So he used the axe. When he hit the stomach, it opened. I turned my head away. Even he wasn't really watching. He turned his head and was retching."

So there you have it, a first hand account, and off they went to drop the body into the depths of Eccleston Quarry. Even that didn't go straightforward.

As Maher drove the car away from the quarry, he scraped the bottom of the car on a rock. Smith and Maher later drove to Scotland.

Maher disposed of the hands in the River Almond at Livingston, following which he flew back to London and Smith disposed of the gun and seat covers. He damaged the gun with a hammer before throwing it into Blackrigg Quarry at Coatbridge.

Smith had abandoned the Jaguar in Airdrie on 15 October after receiving a call from Maher to say that Johnstone's body had been discovered.

Just to remind you, we finished taking the statement from James Smith at 5.10am. Now why did we carry on all night? It was simple really, because he wanted to tell us. He was reliving the experience and I believe to this day that to deny him the opportunity would not have served justice. However, the fact that we had not had any sleep would not come into the equation. I knew that we could be open to possible allegations of duress, oppressive treatment, e.g. denying him sleep; so it was important to try and corroborate what he had said.

I travelled home to Blackpool to freshen up. I was back at Chorley early to fully brief Ray Rimmer and by 11.40am (1 November) we were on the road to Scotland. Our travelling companion was James Smith – he had agreed to come with us to show where he had disposed of material evidence. If we could recover evidence, it would be critical if his written confession was disallowed.

We went to Airdrie Police Station, and then onto Blackrigg Quarry. When we got to the quarry entrance, Detective Sergeant Jack Winskill said, "Whereabouts are the seat covers from the Jag?"

Smith said "They're over there." Indicating a rubbish dump, and there before our very eyes lying quite visible on the dump were two brown seat covers.

Jack Winskill asked, "Are these they?"

Smith replied "Yes".

Smith then took us to the side of the quarry lake and showed us where he had smashed the gun, and where he threw the gun and hammer into the lake.

As I said earlier, luck plays a part. Jack Winskill and George Mitchell stayed to wait for a photographer while we went onto to locate the place where the hands were disposed of. Only 30 minutes after discovery, whilst Jack and George were still waiting for the photographer, they had to stop a lorry tipping a load of rubble at the spot where the seat covers were laying. Now that's the bit of luck you need!

The Strathclyde Police Divers commenced a search of the quarry. At 4.20pm the next day (2 November), which was the first day of their search, PC Hunter came out from under water holding the long hammer Smith had used. We were on the right track.

On our journey back to Chorley, Smith imparted some vital information. Needless to say some of the other members of the team were still denying involvement. We still did not know who had transported the murder weapon. He told us that the person who had brought the gun was a 15- or 16-year-old girl, and not as we had thought the New Zealand barrister girlfriend of Sinclaire.

The day following, Saturday, 3 November, we had an interesting conversation with the trigger man – Andy Maher. We were still trying to find the hands. DS Wright, DC Fleming and I visited Maher. We had a sketch of the River Almond and we wanted him to pinpoint where he had thrown the hands in.

During our conversation he said, "I shouldn't moralise, I know it was planned and premeditated, but I'm not a hit man. I've even started having nightmares about hands coming to get me".

I asked him if he had been a guardsman like Smith. He replied, "No, I was in the marines, but I left after three months. This is going to sound funny coming from me; all they wanted to do was kill people. They're a load of psychos and they get medals for it."

His parting shot was, "… I know it's a laugh, but do you think I'll get off because it's my first offence".

Meanwhile, we had managed to get the Royal Navy Diving Team back in the water to search for the hands. They had done a one-day search without success. We took an underwater Electro-magnet and that got them back in the water. The river had a concrete feature, a modern piece of art, which Smith had referred to; which looked like four fingers appearing out of the water.

On 6 November, I was stood on the banks of the River Almond when Able Seaman Diver Griffiths handed to me a human hand he had found in its waters. I remember it well because DC Fleming had just brought the meat pies for lunch. The hand was in perfect condition and DS Wright took it from me, to take it away for preservation.

Things were not so simple at the Blackrigg Quarry; they had still not found the gun and had searched continually for five weeks. Blackrigg Quarry contained a lot of water and divers were searching in no visibility waters. I paid them a visit and they had this idea for pumping some water out. I was asked if we would pay for the hire of the pump. We did; it was the least we could do. They certainly dropped the level of the water.

They pumped out eleven million gallons of water and flooded every field in sight. Interestingly, no complaint was made by the farmers, or none that we were aware of. On Thursday, 6 December, PC John McCafferky found the gun. It was a tremendous find and the gun was very difficult to see. It was in water and with a tremendous amount of rubbish around it including vehicles which had been dumped. Despite the condition a ballistics expert was able to say that it was likely that the gun had been used to fire the .38 bullet recovered from Johnstone's brain.

James Smith had given us considerable help but even he got a touch of the jitters. He worried about the people he had become involved with, "They're powerful and get anybody," he said.

A CHIEF CONSTABLE'S NIGHTMARE?

But did Smith have any reason to worry? We had heard stories of murders abroad. Several of Clark's associates had ended up murdered.

We had made several trips to Scotland. James Smith had really opened up the case for us. The investigation was pushing on. One day I walked into Ray Rimmer's office, Ray turned to his colleague Phil Cafferky, and said, "That's it Phil, Jeff will go to Singapore for us". I laughed – but it was to be.

My purpose would be to go out immediately to see essential witnesses such as Monique Van Putten, who it was thought, may be in peril. Within 36 hours, with Det Inspector Alan Taylor we were airborne. Because it was feared that there may be attempts on the lives of witnesses in Singapore it was essential to depart as soon as we did. I had the necessary injections from my doctor who informed me I would probably be back in England before they became effective.

I could not tell anyone where I was going until we actually arrived in Singapore. I was due to take an examination with the Open University. I asked Kathy to ring my tutor and explain once I was in Singapore. When Kathy explained, the tutor commented that it sounded like a detective story!

We were met by a Chief Narcotics officer who asked, "Are you from Scotland Yard or the ordinary police?"

I replied, "Neither, we are from the Lancashire Constabulary".

I had a letter from the Chief Constable to present to the High Commissioner. It introduced us and the Chief Constable had written, "I shall be most grateful for any assistance that you are able to afford my officers to facilitate their enquiries".

We arrived at the High Commission and the reception lady asked us if we had an appointment. I said no but it was very important that we see the High Commissioner. We were very quickly ushered in and saw the Acting High Commissioner. He appointed a liaison officer, Brian Watters, the First Secretary. He had at one time served as a police officer. His assistance was invaluable.

We opened safety deposits boxes and recovered certain documents including newspaper cuttings about the death of 'Pommy' Harry Lewis. We interviewed Monique and I have to say it was a very interesting experience carrying out enquiries in Singapore.

We were also asked to join the Commissioner of Singapore Police, Goh Yong Hong and his executive team for lunch at the Cockpit Restaurant. It was a sumptuous Chinese lunch and Alan and I decided as a courtesy to our hosts to use chopsticks. That was a mistake. The Commissioner could see us struggling. He leaned over and said, "Jeffrey, if I were you I would use a fork otherwise these greedy buggers will have eaten it all". We took that advice. The Commissioner was accompanied by his Deputy Michael Chai and four Assistant Commissioners.

I was due to give evidence in another murder trial. Douglas Partington, a 38-year-old engineer was charged with murder and aggravated arson. It was alleged that because he had been jilted by his 20-year-old girlfriend and he wanted revenge. His girlfriend had thought that Partington was separated from his wife, but she learned that he was still living with her and she broke off her relationship with Partington.

In the early hours of one morning, Partington set fire to the girlfriend's house. She was not present but her father and older and younger sisters were. The father broke a front bedroom window to aid his younger daughter's escape. In doing so he sustained a very serious laceration of his right arm which severed a main artery and sadly he bled to death.

It was not my case but I had mentioned that I knew the accused so I went to see him in the cells and chatted about the incident. Because of what he had told me, I had to give evidence. Ray Rimmer telephoned me and said we had to catch an overnight flight back. We were due to land at Heathrow and Ray had sent a car there to get us back to the Crown Court in Preston. However, we were diverted to Prestwich. We hired a car and drove direct to Preston Crown Court.

When I was called in to give my evidence Mr Michael Maguire QC said words to the effect, "You have come a long way to give evidence today".

I replied that I had come from Singapore. Maguire then asked me if I was OK to give evidence and suggested that his Lordship may allow me to sit down on a chair, prompting a groan from the defence barrister. I replied that I was fine and gave my evidence which was quite short. I was asked by the defence counsel if knowing the accused, I had gone in to see him, in the hope that he may confess to someone he knew.

I replied, "Yes". He was not expecting that answer and there was no more cross examination.

Partington was convicted and Mr Justice Hodgson sentenced him to life imprisonment for murder and 12 years for arson which was to run concurrently with the life sentence.

When I got home, Kathy did not seem to be too pleased. She had heard on the radio that we were flying in and I had not told her. I gave her some golden orchids I had bought, her response was she did not like orchids. I had bought her Mum a Chinese Happy Coat, that was not successful either. There was a sort of humph and she said, "My mother is getting divorced". Well you cannot win them all!

Monique subsequently flew to England to provide information; she arrived at Heathrow on 15 December 1979. She was a very interesting character but was never called to give evidence. There were so many enquiries and other officers flew to Los Angeles, USA and to Australia. This was world news and regularly commanded the top spot on the television news.

The committal proceedings took place in May 1980. There are restrictions on reporting at committal in the UK not so for Australia! The newspaper *Age* reported on 30 August 1980 that the Coroner had issued a warrant for the arrest of Clark in connection with the murder of the Wilsons (former associates of Clark). Of course, Clark (Sinclaire) was already in custody in England.

The trial commenced in January. In all there were twelve accused, five of whom were charged with murder, and all twelve were charged with Conspiracy to import controlled drugs and Conspiracy to supply controlled drugs.

The trial judge was Mrs Justice Heilbron. Normally, such trials would be held in the old crown court where the branding iron still remains. However, the trial was held in the Shire Hall. In this Hall all the shields of Lancashire's High Sheriffs are displayed. Major alterations had to be carried out to accommodate the trial.

After a week of legal argument, I was the first police officer called to give evidence. Normally you would have a couple of barristers. In this case, each defendant had a QC with the junior barrister; a misleading term if ever there was one. It is a little disconcerting when there are 24 barristers, many of them making notes of what you say, and you could face questions from any of them. It was necessary to prepare a barristers seating plan.

Special arrangements had to be made for the press and the trial continued until the middle of July; after 115 days and statements from 175 witnesses, all five being convicted of murder. The five were all sentenced to life imprisonment, with a recommendation that Sinclaire and Maher serve a minimum of 20 years. Three of the 12 were acquitted including Sinclaire's barrister girlfriend.

Ray Rimmer was called into the witness box by Mrs Justice Heilbron to receive the highest commendation from the trial judge. The murderers of Johnstone were brought to justice.

Johnstone was a drug trafficker who had enjoyed good times. The pendant he wore had a Chinese inscription 'long life'. Well for him it did not prove correct. He is buried in Chorley Cemetery. As far as Sinclaire was concerned, he had had it all – a fortune with all the trappings. And as for his destiny – he had boasted that, "No prison in the UK can hold me" Well he got that right, but for the wrong reason, He died suddenly following a heart attack in Parkhurst Prison in 1983!

There are theories about his demise and there was a top rated TV documentary *'The Real Mr Asia'* shown in New Zealand in October 2004 which discussed how Clark died. The **'Mr Asia Syndicate'** features in the second series of the Australian true-crime drama *'Underbelly'*, which was broadcast from 9 February 2009 to 4 May 2009.

THE MURDER OF JUDGE WILLIAM OPENSHAW

(Details of this case can be found in *'Murder in Lancashire'* by Alan Sewart,
ISBN 0-7090-3561-6 and in 'Murder Casebook' by Steve Fielding, ISBN 1-85306-325-8.)

We hear much today of so-called miscarriages of justice. In more recent times the police have been portrayed as racist, inept and downright incompetent. What can easily be forgotten is that in the majority of cases, the police do a good job. I'm biased, of course but this case is about another successful murder investigation. A most respected Senior Circuit Judge was brutally murdered in what must be one of the cruellest pre-meditated murders, at the hands of a self-confessed 'monster'.

The story starts about eighteen months before the actual murder. John Smith, then 30 years of age had climbed to the top of Blackpool Tower to make a protest. He attracted widespread publicity, which was his aim. He was, he said, protesting against excessive police powers and conditions within British Prisons.

John Smith had gained access to the pinnacle of the Tower in the early evening of Thursday 14 August 1980 and remained there until he was eventually talked down on the morning of Saturday 16 August 1980.

This was again greeted with front-page headlines. Long negotiations had taken place and a solicitor from Burnley had been called to assist. Smith appeared before the Blackpool Magistrates' Court on 18 August and he agreed to be bound over in the sum of £50 for two years.

Incidentally, my only involvement was that I had watched him from my office window. On the morning of 12 May 1981 I walked into my office. I knew instantly something was wrong. Most of the team were already present and still had their coats on. "The judge has been murdered," someone said. At that time the trial was in progress for the gang members in the 'Handless Corpse or Mr Asia' case. This was a very high profile case which involved some dangerous people. I thought the remark referred to that trial judge. But I thought how could that be? There were armed guards at all times and the Judge had an escort wherever she went.

I was quickly told it was not the trial Judge; we could draw no relief because a most respected Judge had been slain. Judge William Openshaw had been savagely stabbed to death by an assailant who had lain wait in his garage

Ray Rimmer went to the scene and took charge and there was much activity in the vicinity. As it turned out, the man responsible was John Smith who months earlier had made his Tower top protest.

Immediately following the killing, Mr Walter Hide was driving his Austin Maxi car north along the A6 towards the Broughton traffic lights. He was suddenly confronted by Smith who had run into the road, waving his arms frantically. Thinking there was some emergency Mr Hide slowed, whereupon Smith jumped into Mr Hide's car and at knifepoint, forced Mr Hide to drive him on a 130-mile journey.

Smith at one point said to Hide, "I don't suppose you've ever been kidnapped before". It was after that remark, that he gave the reason for killing Judge Openshaw. Smith said, "The guy had it coming to him. About thirteen years ago he sent me down to Borstal".

He made Mr Hide drive to Scotland, eventually stopping when Smith suggested that he should tie Mr Hide to a tree. Smith used jump cables from the car to tie Hide's hands behind him. At one stage Smith actually handed the knife to Hide. Smith then drove off in Hide's Maxi and said he would phone shortly to get him released.

Mr Hide managed to escape and the police were informed. Constables Henderson and Nicol attempted a road block but Henderson had to leap out of the path of the car driven by Smith. His colleague gave chase, forcing Smith to stop. Smith abandoned the car and ran across a field where Constables Wilson and Smith pursued him. Constable Wilson brought Smith to the ground whilst Constable Smith removed a knife from John Smith's waistband.

Smith was placed in custody and when he appeared at Jedburgh Court, the man who craved publicity had his head covered in a blanket. Ray Rimmer asked me to go to Scotland to bring him back – I went with Mike Arnold (then a Detective Constable) and I was to take the Divisional Detective Inspector Roy Slater, who was off duty.

I called round at Roy's home. He was up a ladder painting; "Will I be long?" he asked, "No" I replied – and didn't we get that one wrong. When we got Scotland we found out that the

Lothian and Borders Police had charged Smith with kidnapping Mr Hyde at Carter Bar. But we did interview Smith and it was quite an interview:

It was quite a long interview and at first he said his mind was a blank. He admitted threatening Hide with a knife and then he referred to the Tower incident, "What I wanted (was) to tell everyone about politicians and the system and police brutality. Blokes like me aren't given a chance."

I examined his hands. He had a slight abrasion.

DCI: "How did you get that?"
Smith: "Scrapping."
DCI: "How do you mean, fighting?"
Smith: "No the metal job."
DCI: I kept hold of his hands and looked at him.
Smith: "What are you looking at those for, what are you trying to prove?"
DCI: "What have these hands done today John, what have they done?"

He did not reply.

He looked at his hands and started to perspire:

DCI: "You've started to sweat John, what's the matter. Tell me what these hands have done today"

It was at this point that he confessed and when asked why he had done it:

Smith: "Because he was the bastard who sent me down the first time on five charges, unauthorised taking, housebreaking and shopbreaking. I remember the day. It was a leap year. It was 29 February

He later said that it was between Judge Openshaw and Judge Kershaw, adding that he had politicians on the list; his rationale: "Politicians make the law, judges enforce it. They are all pillocks"

He also added, "If I ever get out of here you had better watch it."

DCI: "What me personally?"

He said, "No, the top policemen like McNee and Anderton. It's the only way to get publicity. That's why I decided on the judge first."

He harked back to when he was up the Tower, saying, "…It's like Blackpool people just don't comprehend. While I was up that tower kids wrote 'jump' in the sand, but I'm not that fucking daft. If I'd done that the only people who would have gained were the civil liberties and people like them, who would have played on my predicament. I've thought this all out, I knew I would never see the light of day again, I knew I couldn't win. In some respects he's better off than I am."

DCI:	"So you've been thinking about this for a long time?"
Smith:	"I know what you're after."
DCI:	"What?"
Smith:	"You're after my state of mind."
DCI	"How do you mean?"
Smith:	"There are several things open to me."
DCI:	"Such as?"
Smith:	"Diminished responsibility," and at this point he smiled.
DCI:	"Have you been getting messages as well?" (This was a reference to the Yorkshire Ripper Trial – Sutcliffe claimed he received messages)

Smith laughed at this point and said,

	"Not from fucking God like the other one. You're not talking to a mug. I've been doing plenty of reading. They might accept the American system where the state of the mind can go back for years."
DCI:	"Why kill an old man?"
Smith:	"To get my protest over. Killing another human being is the most serious offence of all. That will get me more publicity."

He later wrote out his own statement of confession, in which he described the murder: He had arrived at 2.30am and looked for somewhere to hide, selecting eventually the beams of the garage.

> "...I took up my position at around 4.30 – before that I'd seen an old hut and decided to try and catch a few hour's sleep, it was cold – however I couldn't sleep, after I took up my position on the beams I then waited for morning, the reason I went up so early was because I didn't know the time he would be coming out to leave, I was kept waiting until around 7.30 (am) when I heard the paperboy or somebody on a bike delivering papers or milk – it was about 8.30 next when I heard a door bang – I thought it was him but it must have been someone else as they left quickly – the reason I'm telling you all this is because from where I was I couldn't see anyone – the next sound I heard was of someone banging the door and walking slowly towards the garage. I knew it had to be him so I got ready. When he was passing under me I decided against jumping on him as I didn't want to get him in the back, I wanted to see his face and expressions on it when I confronted him; when he passed and (was) opening the car door I jumped down. I pulled my sheaf knife out from my waistband and drew the knife, he just looked at me startled and didn't know what to say, I then approached him and said, "Now then I've got you" – he replied something – "oh no please" – I lunged at him..."

He then described in some detail, how he repeatedly stabbed the Judge, inflicting the fatal stab wounds. When we were driving back, Smith said a few interesting things, not least of which was, "Why did he have to send me down in '68. If he hadn't, he could still be alive today and I wouldn't be the monster I am".

And a parting shot from him was "... nobody is fair to me. Even the fellow I highjacked broke his promise to me. He said he wouldn't try to free himself, but he did. I could have killed him couldn't, I but I didn't want to. I trusted him. I even gave him my knife to cut the wire I tied him up with."

And then he made another comment saying he would not plead 'not guilty' because, "I'm not going to cause that Openshaw widow any more distress. I don't want her giving evidence."

Smith was arrested as he was still 'in flight' on the day of the murder 12 May, 1981. At a magistrates' court hearing on 28 May, Smith's solicitor revealed that on the instructions of Smith, he had gone to Burnley, where under the floorboards he recovered a statement which he must have prepared before the murder, which according to the solicitor, indicated Smith's state of mind then, and indicated what he was about to do and his reason.

Smith's trial was at Leeds Crown Court. Well I have to say it was not your normal trial. He refused to recognise the court, had sacked two barristers and was represented by Mr Ivan Lawrence QC who also was dismissed by Smith during the trial. I was called in to give evidence to determine whether he was mute by malice or act of God. As I walked into the courtroom, I looked into the dock, but could not see Smith who was sat down on the dock floor, but I certainly heard him.

As I passed by he shouted, "Tell the truth Meadows, it'll be the first time, you're a fucking cowboy". Now this was a man who was supposed to be mute. I gave evidence and the jury very quickly determined that he was mute by malice.

A new jury was empanelled and Smith continued to behave by interrupting. Every now and then, he would look to the public gallery and shout to his sister, "What's happening Brenda?" No witness was cross-examined and I read out to the court his own statement of confession, which he had written in his own handwriting.

He was convicted of the murder and the unlawful imprisonment of Mr Hide by a majority verdict – 10 to two. This I found difficult to understand.

Smith then wanted the statement found under the floorboards read out. Mr Justice Lawson agreed but warned, "I'm not going to allow this court to be used for his attention-seeking activities. He is a dangerous man."

Smith shouted, "You are going to humiliate and degrade people, aren't you sadist," he told the judge, as two prison officers hauled him to his feet to listen to the passing of the sentence.

On the first charge he was sentenced to life imprisonment with a direction that he should serve a minimum of twenty-five years, and on the second to five year's imprisonment, to run concurrently.

'I won't forget you,' he shouted to Judge Lawson as he was being taken from the dock. 'I'll cut your throat when I get out'.

And, typically, he had yet another last word, "I am not sorry for what I have done, I would do the same again tomorrow".

Smith said to me, "I want the world's press at court. Well the nationals anyway. I want to get over my point of view".

Well he got over his point of view – the cost – the death of an honourable man.

MURDER OF ARTHUR BANKS, SCHOOL ROAD, BLACKPOOL

26th MARCH 1980

Arthur Banks was 79 years old and ran a shop in School Road, Marton an area of Blackpool, it was no ordinary shop. In some ways it was as though you were being transported back through a time warp. One sometimes felt that it belonged to another age. He sold everything you could think of. It was across the road from St Nicholas' Primary School and for the children was their favourite tuck shop. Some of the children called him Uncle Arthur.

Sadly Arthur was the subject of a violent robbery as a result of which he died. The offenders had tied a towel round his face and he died from asphyxiation.

The murder room was set up in the school. The one thing this enquiry revealed is that villains had their own 'departments'. What we learned was that because it was thought there would be a significant amount of cash on the premises, the 'conmen' team would be used. However, Arthur was too alert to fall for any fraudster's trick, so it was thought that someone would be recruited to carry out a burglary. The problem was that Arthur very rarely went out. Eventually they decided on the 'heavy team', and three men travelled from Leeds and carried out the fateful attack and robbery.

Enquiries progressed resulting in the identity and location of the three suspects. A team was assembled and a group of officers allocated to each suspect and off we went to Leeds in the early hours of one morning. I led one group and my colleagues Detective Chief Inspector John Boyd and Detective Inspector Harry Maylor led the other two groups. The men were arrested and brought back to Blackpool where after questioning they were charged with the death of Arthur Banks. This enquiry also led the police to prolific receivers of stolen property in the East Lancashire area.

The trial was very interesting. Giving evidence were two Detective Superintendents, four Detective Chief Inspectors and about 20 other detectives. When you are going to give evidence you have an idea of the 'batting order' and it was likely that I would follow Detective Superintendent Norman Finnerty. However, much to Norman's surprise, I was called in first. I gave my evidence in chief, then a barrister defending the accused whose interview I had been involved in, said words to the effect, "Now I would like to take you into matters not covered by your deposition".

The defence were alleging that some remark had been made by a detective. Apparently if this remark had been made, it could affect the quality of other evidence. I told the defence barrister I had not made such a remark and I did not hear anyone else make it. The High Court Judge, if my memory is correct it was Mr Justice McNeill, said, "I know you are not the officer in charge of the case but you are a senior Lancashire CID Officer," or words to that effect. I responded saying to His Lordship that I did not want to mislead the court on something of which I had no knowledge. The judge called an usher and I was told to be kept separate from any other officer. I had to go for lunch on my own and under no circumstances had I to contact or speak to any other detective involved in the case. The three offenders were subsequently convicted and jailed.

The stars of this investigation for me were the members of the No 1 District Task Force Dog Section. A small piece of rubber glove had been found in Mr Bank's shop. It was decided that the return route taken by the offenders would be searched. This meant that searching a country road and then east along the M55, south along the M6 and east along the M61 motorways.

Sergeant Brian Smith and Jack Heartwell supervised the search and just before junction eight on the M61 motorway, dog handler Sam McNeillie found a rubber glove. Scientists were able to show conclusively that the fragment in the shop matched the rubber glove found by Sam.

The dog team had worked most of April and covered about 30 miles in difficult circumstances. This was brilliant and dedicated police work.

AN ENCOUNTER WITH THE CHINESE TRIADS

A robbery at the home of a Chinese Restaurant Owner led to a major enquiry. The restaurateur and his family were tied up and bound by a Chinese gang. It transpired that restaurant owners in various parts of the country had been robbed by men armed with long knives and axes. Some quite serious injuries had been inflicted on the unfortunate victims. The Task Force CID led by Detective Superintendent Norman Finnerty gave support to Divisional Detectives

In trying to solve our own robbery (which we never did) we started to make enquiries. We knew that Manchester had a big Chinese Community, so we liaised with our colleagues in Greater Manchester Police. Starting from basics, we ascertained which individuals had criminal convictions or associated with criminals. I took a team of Divisional and Task Force detectives to Manchester and we were given an office to work from. Officers were paired up and went to various restaurants etc., and brought in likely suspects. It was not always straightforward. On one occasion Detective Sergeant (later DCI) Brian McVittie and the late Detective Constable Ian Green were chased out of a restaurant by a cleaver waving Chinese man, but being sound detectives they did arrest him.

At one stage we had several Chinese men in custody, what they did not know was that we had an 'ace up our sleeve', we had taken PC Paul O'Connor with us. Paul, a beat Bobby from Blackpool had been brought up in Hong Kong and was a former Merchant Navy Officer. He spoke fluent Cantonese with a little Mandarin. One of the problems we faced was that the suspects were claiming they could not speak or understand English. I asked Paul if he fancied playing the sleepy drunk in a cell. He readily agreed and he was put in a holding cell with some of the suspects.

When we got the suspects back to Blackpool, they persisted in not being able to speak or understand English, at that point we brought Paul into them. He spoke to them in Cantonese and they were truly shocked. It transpired that the majority could speak and understand the English language.

Now there may be some raised eyebrows at the ploy we used, putting Paul in the cells with the suspects. Police officers are sometimes properly criticised for the way they have behaved. I used to lecture on the Home Office Detective Training Course – my topic the use and dangers of police informants. You can never act as 'agent provocateur'.

However, I do believe though that as investigating officers there are boundaries both moral and legal, beyond which we must not trespass. But conscious of our duty to thoroughly and vigorously investigate crime, the occasional use of subtlety is not improper. Obviously the defence team would be told by their clients what had transpired but it did not become an issue.

We kept the accused men in custody, it was a difficult situation because there were problems with the prisons and Operation Container was running. This meant that the prisoners who normally went to a Remand Centre had to be detained locally. The custody officers generally got on well with the prisoners and I did not want our officers to 'lower their guard' so I spoke to the late Inspector Jack Nelson who was running Operation Container. Some of the prisoners had admitted membership of the Chinese Triads, notably 14K and Wo Shing Wo. I showed Jack some photographs sent by the Metropolitan Police, which showed some horrendous injuries inflicted and we suspected, by some of those detained.

At one hearing at the magistrates' court we were applying for custody when the father of one of the accused offered me money to get his son bail. I mentioned it to my friend Sam Lee who was representing the son. Sam just smiled and said, "That's what's they do," or words to that effect. I warned the father not to try that again or he would face serious consequences.

The defendants, who were charged with offences in Preston, Huddersfield, Poynton in Cheshire, Hadfield in Derbyshire and Wakefield, came to respect Paul. There were nine accused who were charged with offences, which included aggravated burglary, robbery and other offences but not all of them faced the same charge. They all pleaded guilty and were given custodial sentences.

Some actually asked me if Paul could be the interpreter at their trial. Of course, that could not happen. In sentencing them, the Judge said that he was sentencing them on the nature of the offences and was not taking into consideration whether they were or were not members of the Triads. The activities of these gang members had been brought to an end, but of course, there are always others waiting to replace them.

Paul O'Connor's prosecution statement ran to 172 pages, that meant a lot more typing for Linda Cawley. Paul's contribution to the success of the enquiries was immense, I am quite sure that without Paul's input, many of those detained would have escaped justice.

Jeff leading Land of Hope and Glory

Darren & Jeff

Jeff's graduation

Welbeck

Mersey Tunnel - Going in the wrong way

Jeff at Highfield

Darren and Anne's wedding

Ken Wilkinson's sketch of Motorway Seminar team

Another Ken Wilkinson's sketch of Motorway Seminar team

LANCASHIRE CONSTABULARY

Secretariat.
2nd February 1988.

MEMORANDUM TO CHIEF SUPERINTENDENT, OPERATIONS

Re. Motorway Seminar - 30th/31st January 1988

I write to place on record my deep appreciation for the splendid organisation and enthusiasm you brought to the recent Seminar.

~~While the Force basks in the reflected glory, it should be placed~~ on record that the idea came from you and that you have had total responsibility for the programming, the speakers and making all the necessary arrangements.

I know the tremendous amount of work that must have gone into making this a success and those present could not fail to have been impressed with the organisation of the event and with the readiness of all your officers to help and assist the delegates in any way they could.

As I said at the Seminar, the weekend was an unqualified success and I would be grateful if you could pass on to all your officers my thanks and the thanks of the Force for their splendid efforts.

Brian Johnson
Chief Constable.

Letter from Chief re Motorway Safety Campaign

Accident investigation Team

Airship at Cardington

Prince Charles visits new Communication Room

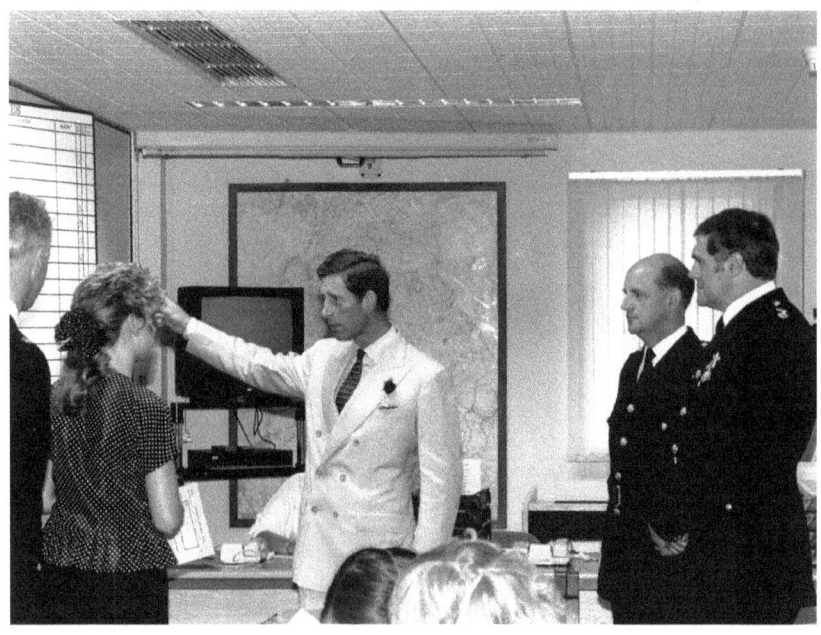

Prince Charles visits new Communication Room

Queen at Whitewell - Waving goodbye to tenant farmers

Queen at Whitewell - Jeff waving convoy through

Queen at Whitewell - Kathy at the reception

Chief and Jeff with Prince Charles

Farewell to the Duke of Kent

Greeting Princess Anne

Greeting Princess Alexandra

Jeff looking after Princess Margaret

HM Queen leaving from Blackpool Airport

Jeff chats to the motorcyclists

Jeff meets John Major

Ken and Jeff

Final Evening Gazette

THURSDAY, APRIL 16, 1992   No. 19448   *Putting the Fylde First*

PLAY THE £30,000 BREAKFAST GAMBLE   see page 3

'ELLO 'ELLO

Flat-out – and copped!

CUT-OUT COPS: the dummy police vehicle which was spotted on the M55 hard-shoulder

By JOHN MANGNALL

DUMMY police cars are being tested on Lancashire's motorways in an experiment to reduce speeding.

Police and road safety experts are working together to gauge motorists' reactions to fibre glass cut-outs of police Range Rovers.

But they say it is a serious, low-profile evaluation and want to avoid the kind of derisive publicity attracted in the North East when police put cardboard cut-outs of police vehicles on motorway bridges.

Chief Superintendent Jeff Meadows, head of Lancashire's traffic and uniformed operations department, said: "We are liaising with the Transport Research Laboratory in the evaluation of a traffic calming sign to reduce speed.

"And we are doing it under very strict scientific control."

The model was spotted on a police vantage point on the M55 near the Kirkham turn off yesterday but today it had been moved to another stretch of motorway.

One motorist who passed the model said: "It looked very realistic and it was only when I got close that I realised it was a cut out.

"It certainly made people slow down. I think it is a good idea to curb motorway speeders."

Mr Meadows said Lancashire was not following the lead of any other police force.

"We have been looking at this project for more than 12 months," he said.

"We are testing the model and there is nothing significant about it being used during the Easter holiday. It is just part of the research programme."

He added: "We knew it would be spotted but it may be there is to be a further evaluation period."

The project has been given the thumbs-up by motoring organisation the RAC.

A spokesman said: "I think this might be the road to go down because there is evidence that these models do have a calming effect.

"The cardboard cut-out scheme in the North East caused a stir but early reports suggest that people do slow down."

Whirlwind

Jeff with Linda Lusardi

WARWICKSHIRE CONSTABULARY
Chief Constable: Peter D. Joslin, Q.P.M., B.A., C.B.I.M.

Telephone: Warwick (0926) 415000
Telex: 31548 (POWARK)
Fax: Warwick (0926) 50362

Police Headquarters,
P.O. Box 4,
Leek Wootton,
Warwick CV35 7QB

PDJ/PMT/4
20th August 1991

PERSONAL

R. B. Johnson, Esq., CBE, QPM, DL,
Chief Constable,
Lancashire Constabulary,
PO Box 77,
Hutton,
Nr. Preston,
Lancashire PR4 5SB

Dear Brian,

CHIEF SUPERINTENDENT J. MEADOWS

Now that the 1991 Police National Motorway Safety Campaign is over, I felt I must write to you to say how impressed I was with the way in which Chief Superintendent MEADOWS carried out his role as Secretary of the Campaign Committee. His traffic experience, his energy and his commitment were an example to all and made a tremendous contribution to the success of the campaign.

It is not easy, as you know, to pull together the efforts of so many Police Forces as well as outside organisations and the cheerful way in which he undertook his task resulted in a highly professional organisation with the minimum of conflict. There were times when he showed that he was not afraid to resolve difficult problems forcibly and throughout he displayed an extremely high quality of leadership.

May I thank you personally for allowing Jeff MEADOWS to spend so much of his time on the campaign and I would be very grateful if you could convey my thanks to him. You may feel that the credit that he brought on the Lancashire Constabulary and the Police Service as a whole is worthy of commendation.

Yours sincerely,

Peter D. Joslin
Chief Constable

Letter from CC Peter Joslin

Queen's Police Medal Investiture for distinguished police service

Thomas, Jeff and Benjamin at QPM Investiture

My Superintendants at the Investiture, John Mallalieu, Roy Hutching and Bernard Kershaw

Derek McNamara, Jeff and Ken Mackay at the Investiture

Group picture at the Investiture

Kathy, Thomas and Benjamin in the Chief's car

CHAPTER ELEVEN

A CROWN ON MY SHOULDER AND LATER, A PIP TO GO WITH IT

October 1982 saw me promoted to Superintendent. You never know what is around the corner, I enjoyed my time as Detective Chief Inspector and the then Head of CID sounded me out about taking on the role of Divisional Detective Superintendent. However, the then Deputy Chief Constable Brian Johnson called me in, the Divisional Detective Superintendent's post had gone to another officer a couple of weeks earlier.

"Was I disappointed that I had not got that job?" he asked.

I could answer quite honestly that I wasn't disappointed, just pleased I had been considered. We chatted for a while and Mr Johnson then said that he would like me to work for him as a Superintendent in Discipline and Complaints at HQ (now called Professional Standards). I was to be the only full-time investigator although divisional senior officers were also allocated enquiries.

The nature of the work means that I cannot talk about that period. I had been told that I would be in that post for two years and I got to know Mr Johnson really well, which was no bad thing because he later became Chief Constable of Lancashire Constabulary.

On 11 June 1983, I graduated from the Open University with a Bachelor of Arts Degree; I had majored in politics and my tutor, now a professor at Lancaster University asked if I would consider applying to undertake a Master's Degree at Lancaster University. I reminded him that I had not gone on for honours because of the demands of the job. He said that being a mature student, I could be accepted on interview and he was optimistic that I would be accepted. I declined this offer because my family had put up with quite a lot with me being ensconced in a room studying, it would have been interesting to take it on but I have no regrets that I did not.

Between 25 June and 13 September 1984, I attended the Intermediate Command Course (for Superintendent rank) at Bramshill House, the National Police Staff College. I enjoyed the course and according to Brian Johnson who was then Chief Constable, did very well. Mr Johnson was true to his word and two years later, I was appointed Sub-Divisional Commander at Blackpool South Sub-Division. This was bliss – in charge of my home patch.

At that time the National Miners' Strike was in full flow. Officers on their Rest Days were being sent to Yorkshire and it became evident to me that some were becoming fatigued. We also had to ensure as far as we could, that officers and their families were not getting used to the big pay packets and creating problems for the future.

I checked the 'time in' book and was horrified to see that if the sub-divisional personnel took all their time off, we would have no sub-divisional cover for January, February and March! Things had to change and I introduced a system whereby the 6am to 2pm shift would work 6am to 6pm and the night shift would work 6pm to 6am. This left the 2pm to 10pm shift free to be deployed for duty in connection with the Miners' Strike. This meant there should be less fatigue; everyone would still get overtime, albeit reduced and importantly all had to take their rest days.

This was not a popular decision and there were grumblings. I felt a little sorry for the constable delegated by his colleagues to come and speak to me. He told me he was there 'on behalf of the lads' who were 'not very happy'. I handed him the overtime book and asked him to study it and tell me what he would do, he looked at it and said words to the effect, 'I don't know what to do". I told him I did and that was why the new system was introduced. I also suggested that he should have had a word with his sergeants or officers. I suspect, however that he had already done that and he had been told to come and see me!

I did not escape involvement in the Miners' Strike. It appeared that the Nottingham Superintendents needed mutual aid from Superintendents from other forces. I was sent to Welbeck Colliery in Nottingham (on a visit to Warner's Thoresby Hall Hotel in retirement, I noticed the signs to Welbeck Colliery. I had not realised it was so close to the Hotel).

I was at Welbeck for one week and I had responsibility for looking after the Colliery and Village. I had two support units, one from Essex and one from Hampshire. They were good officers and each contingent had an Inspector in charge. The miners appeared to be anti-Arthur Scargill and wanted to work. They later formed The Union of Democratic Mineworkers but coal mining at the pit ceased in 2010.

The week passed without incident. They were really anti-social shifts – commencing at about 1am and finishing at noon the next day. Everyone was given a full English breakfast. I dined with George the Pit Deputy Manager. My first breakfast was absolute huge and drew comments from the troops so I asked George to give me the same breakfast as the troops, which was in fact a good breakfast. George also arranged for everyone who wished to to have a trip down the mine when they were off duty.

Welbeck was said to be one of the most modern pits in Europe. When I went down the mine, I did not enjoy the ride on the little railway because I had to virtually lay flat. It was not a pleasant experience, and it made me think of my little granddad Patrick Horrocks, who was miner and worked in the Haig Pit, Whitehaven, which went some four and a half miles under the sea.

I was very fortunate because local community Bobbies were allocated to each shift, the liaison constable with me was a mine of information (pardon the pun) and great to work with.

A CHIEF CONSTABLE'S NIGHTMARE?

The one date which stays in my mind was 12 October 1984, when a bomb exploded in the Grand Hotel, Brighton during the Conservative Conference, killing five people and injuring 34 others, some very seriously. I remember watching the aftermath on a television set in the Colliery Office. You think of the dead and injured, but what was also in my mind was that Blackpool was to host the next conference. The explosion occurred about 2.45am. That incident was going to have a big impact on what was to come.

Our pre-planning for the Conservative Conference in 1985 went into full speed. I had a meeting with Assistant Chief Constable Mike Prunty who said he would like me to become Venue Commander for the Imperial Hotel. This was a great challenge because many members of the Government would be staying there. With my deputy DCI Dave Taylorson we started to plan, meeting up with military experts and colleagues in other forces. Between 5 and 7 February 1985 we visited colleagues in the Metropolitan Police at New Scotland Yard who were very helpful. One comment was, "You've got so much time you'll create a monster". I remember thinking, "Well this attack on the Government has certainly encouraged cooperation between forces".

Towards the end of 1984 I had to have a chat with the Chief, he said he would be making some moves and asked me if I would consider a second-in-command role of a division. I said I would consider it and he told me to go and chat with Mike Prunty, which I did. I discussed it with Kathy and went back to see Mike Prunty. I told him that, 'I would throw my hat into the ring'. He then suggested I attend the Extended Interview Board which prepares officers for Chief Officer Ranks. After some thought, I agreed.

Within four months I was called into to see the Chief who told me that he was promoting me to Chief Superintendent to take command of the Traffic and Uniform Operations Department. So a pip was added underneath the crown on my uniform and epaulettes. The Chief said that it was my job for 'a couple of years'. I stayed in that role for over ten years, it was a very busy, challenging and thoroughly enjoyable ten years. It follows that in reality, I can only give a snapshot of those ten years. My responsibilities were well outlined in the Chief Constable' Annual Report of 1993 (page 23).

> *"The Operations (Traffic and Uniform) Department covers a wide variety of policing functions and provides support to Divisions in both planned and unplanned operational policing events. The work of the department can be broadly divided into five inter-related areas.* **MANAGEMENT AND CO-ORDINATION** *involves various branches of the Department working to the Chief Superintendent (Traffic and Uniform) who with his senior colleagues has the responsibility for planning and co-ordinating major policing events which go beyond the resources of one division, e.g. Royal Visits, and political conferences; the* **COMMAND** *element of the Mounted Branch, Motorway Group and the Support Unit in providing operational cover across the county; the* **SERVICE** *function provides a force wide communication system along with other specialist services including Underwater Search, Traffic Management and Accident Investigation as well as technical equipment back up;* **POLICY AND MONITORING** *formulates policy on traffic and uniform matters and creates and maintains contingency plans; integrated in all these is the* **ADMINISTRATION** *function which provides support for the whole department".*

So here I am, Head of the Traffic and Uniform Operations Department; quite humorous when you consider I once tried to drive through the Mersey Tunnel by entering the exit lane on the Liverpool side. The signs had confused me; well that's my reason but I used the experience when giving a presentation to draw attention to situations where there were too many signs which could confuse the driver. Colleague David Jones drew a cartoon depicting my experience at the Mersey Tunnel. I found that the use of a humorous slide could often get the point over. In the early days I also had responsibility for the Vehicle Workshop but this was later transferred to the Administration Department. I got tremendous support from the Chief Engineer and the engineers in the Radio Branch. There were approximately 60 engineers.

The previous Chief Superintendent had retired several weeks before I took over Traffic and Uniform Operations, it was a new world for me but I had very good support. My deputy was Superintendent Trevor Stone, an experienced Traffic Officer, he was very welcoming and a loyal and excellent support to me. Sergeant Bill Smith was in charge of the large admin office, he was a delightful man who was a very supportive to me. Chief Inspector Brian Thoburn who sat in the office next door was the man responsible for the efficient running of my office. I had worked with Brian when we were both at Blackpool, he was good to work with and then we had the ladies in the administration office. Brian's role was civilianised and until my retirement I had two very good secretaries, Diane and Sandra and a top civilian team. All the Operation lasses were an invaluable part of the team.

Of course we had to prepare for the Political Conferences but on promotion to Chief Superintendent, my role changed to a coordinating role. Venue commanders were given ownership and with their team, they had to produce a plan how they would police and secure their venues. They then submitted their plan to Headquarters and my team had the responsibility to the overall commander, to ensure everything had been covered. The plans were kept extremely confidential and will not be discussed here. In the early days I was appointed Deputy Overall Commander during the Conferences, working 8pm to 8am and the overall commander worked 8am to 8pm, but he was always contactable.

Over the years we developed very good liaison with the military and Dorset and Sussex Police who also hosted Political Conferences. We each visited one another's conferences. It was a continual learning process.

I was very pleased to be invited back to my old school, Highfield High School on 17 June 1985, to speak and present awards at the Speech Day. I took the opportunity to remind the students of the ultimate sacrifice by a former pupil Colin Morrison, 38 years, a traffic officer who along with two other colleagues, Angela Bradley 24 years, and Gordon Connolly 23 years, perished in the sea trying to save 25-year-old Alistair Anthony who had gone into the sea to save his dog. Mr Anthony also perished.

In a special report in *The Gazette* on 4 January 2008, *Gazette* features writer Jacqui Morley wrote "... Survivor PC Pat Abrams, who retired 18 months ago, saw traffic Bobby Morrison flash past, through a red light, siren screaming, at Talbot Square. Pat, with just minutes to go before his shift ended, joined PC Gordon Connolly, 24, and WPC Angela Bradley, 25, racing to the Middle Walk. They roped up, Pat wearing the lifebelt, in their first attempt to reach Alistair. Pat entered the sea and got within six feet but the line fell short. They returned to the slade then made the fateful decision to try again, Gordon holding on to the lifeline, which Angela had wrapped around her waist, and Pat wearing the lifebelt. A rogue wave swept them off their feet. Pat went under and was banged against the wall. He came up to see Angela being buffeted against the wall. Gordon was near her. 'I never saw him again.' Then he saw a day-glo jacket in the water. 'It was Colin Morrison. He was in a bad way. He gasped: "We're done for."' Pat told him to hang on, the lifeboat was coming. He fought to keep a grip on Colin, fully clothed and heavy, and offered him the lifebelt. 'But Colin said, "no, just keep me up."' A statement to the inquest, with Pat still in hospital, told how the struggle ended when he realised he was holding a dead man afloat. Pat was hauled from the sea by the lifeline tangled around his neck. The risk of strangulation, even a broken neck, was deemed an acceptable risk. Medics failed to find a pulse and fought to revive him. They included Dr John Frankland, a cave rescue expert who just happened to be passing on his way home to Lancaster. PC Martin Hewitson, 28, was also battered by the waves as he went to the bottom of the slade to throw a lifebelt to the group in the water. He was later hospitalised for shock. For three hours, the Fleetwood lifeboat could not get within 75 yards of the seawall, while the inflatable dinghy which replaced Blackpool's lifeboat three years earlier couldn't be launched. PC Morrison's body was recovered by a winchman lowered from a helicopter. Angela's body was recovered from a sandbank at Preesall days later and Mr Anthony's body was found at Knott End on 14 January. PC Connolly was not found until 27 January. The tragedy shocked the resort and made news around the world...".

The tragedy occurred on the 5th January 1983 and every year we gather at Gynn Square on that day to remember our fallen colleagues.

I had not been in post long when the Chief called me in to say that I was to take over Royal Visits which was previously in Special Branch's domain. The Annexe contains a list of all the Royal Visits I was involved in. There was over 50 and on all but a couple of occasions when away on the day of the visit, I was on duty during the visits. On the occasions I was not on duty on the visit, I was still very much involved in the planning.

The Chief called me one day to tell me that he was introducing a Support Unit; there were similar groups in existence e.g. Special Patrol Group in the Met, Tactical Aid Group in Greater Manchester. The Lancashire scheme would see a Chief Inspector in command with an inspector and team to cover the eastern side of the County and an Inspector and team to cover the western side. I had to select the officers, which I did. It was a very successful outfit, they were extremely well trained.

The Support Unit were often in demand to assist divisions. I was sat at home one evening and was reading *The Gazette*, the local daily paper. There were banner headlines on the front page, 'POLICE CHIEF PROMISES A RING OF STEEL' or similar words. As soon as I saw it, I thought that sounds like my pal Chief

Superintendent Ken Mackay, he was expecting many travellers to try and park on the Blackpool South Shore car park. The previous year there had been considerable disorder. I thought he'll be ringing me in the morning.

When I got into my office the next morning; the early call came from Ken. He asked me if I could let him have some Support Unit officers. I was pleased to help him out.

Between 23 and 26 November, I attended the Extended Interview Board at Eastbourne. It was not an unpleasant experience. You are allowed three attempts, I was not successful and was encouraged to go again. However, I thought long and hard and decided not to, one thing that influenced me was the fact that when Kathy's mother died she was supported enormously by family and friends who would call in to see her. Did I want to take her to some new force in a strange area? The answer was no. But there was also a professional reason; obviously you could not pick and choose and I could not see myself serving as Assistant Chief Constable in Administration or Community Affairs. I spoke to the Chief. He accepted my decision but said if I changed my mind, I would get 100% support from him.

In January 1986, Darren joined Greater Manchester police (GMP) as a constable. It was a nice day when Kathy and I attended Darren's Passing Out Parade at Bruche District Police Training Centre. Another Meadows was a Bobby!

Darren was posted to the C Division, Grey Mare Lane police station, Beswick Manchester and would remain there for the next 10 years working both as a uniform and detective constable. On 9 May 1987, Darren married Ann Barnes at Marton United Reformed Church in Blackpool. Music was provided by David Miller, Head of Music at St George's School and young singers and musicians from the school.

I represented the Constabulary on several Regional and National Conferences. I was on the ACPO National Motorway Conference, this was a sub-committee of the ACPO Traffic

Committee. Our role was to deal with any matters passed down from the senior committee and also generally give informed advice about matters relating to motorway driving and safety. I attended my first meeting on 16 May 1985 and served till my retirement, being Chairman for the last five years.

I was also on the ACPO Speed Detection Group for ten years, my first meeting being on 22 May 1985. I know this will not make me universally popular but following two European Research Tours, we laid the ground work for the introduction of the Speed Cameras. Between 29 March and 1 April 1987 together with other members of the ACPO Standing Committee for Speed Detection (later renamed the ACPO Standing Sub-Committee on Traffic Enforcement Technology), I visited Baden Wurttemberg to examine how their police dealt with speeding and driving to close. They operated with automatic equipment, and it was a very useful experience.

In the two year period 1985/1987 there was three major accidents on the Lancashire Motorways M6 and M61. One involved a coach on the M6 on 21 October 1985 and resulted in 13 deaths. On 28 October 1987 a diesel tanker truck was involved in a collision which resulted in a similar number of fatalities and a minibus was involved in an accident on the M6 near Lancaster and eight people died.

I chatted to the Chief about the carnage and what could we do, I suggested that we should organise an international conference. The Chief liked the idea and arrangements were put in progress. I reminded him that the police from Baden Wurttemberg had demonstrated their speed detection equipment previously. We contacted them and they agreed to send officers over with the equipment worth about a quarter of a million pounds. Now it might have been my suggestion, but I had an excellent team headed by Superintendent John Mallalieu working on the organisation.

The date was set – 30/31 January 1988 and the Police Authority approved the use of the Training School to provide food and accommodation. This was agreed because many potential speakers would probably be booked midweek but could be free at the weekend. That decision proved to be correct as we had a full house with various road safety experts and interested professionals. I had a great team with John, David Taylor, Ken Wilkinson and Mrs Jackie King. Ken was a talented artist and drew two sketches of our team.

The seminar was a great success and we sent a report to the Minister for Road and Traffic. In the Chief's annual report for 1988 he commented, *"In April the Secretary of State for Transport published a package of measures designed to improve motorway safety and it was pleasing to note that many of these were similar to those recommended in the Constabulary report"*. I am so grateful to the Motorway Safety Seminar Team and particularly to John Mallalieu who wrote the report.

On 28 April 1988, our first grandson Benjamin Jeffrey Meadows was born. It was a shock to Kathy who said that she was not ready to be a Grandma. I said, "What about me having to sleep with a Granny"!

With the support of the *Lancashire Evening Post* (LEP) we started the ENOUGH IS ENOUGH campaign and introduced a system of prosecuting motorists who flouted the 50mph speed limits in the road works. It was national news because we recorded the speed and details of the offending vehicles. We did not stop the motorist, the first indication for an offender was a summons dropping through the post. The LEP published the names of all the offenders, before we started, we publicised what we were intending to do. The campaign was on regional TV and I even appeared on Pebble Mill.

One of the projects we undertook whilst on the ACPO National Motorway Conference (a subcommittee of the Association of Chief Police Officers' Traffic Committee) was the introduction of the 'Battenberg' livery on police vehicles. We had to identify a livery which would be conspicuous and readily identifiable as a police vehicle. I set up a working group led by Superintendent Derek Bristow of Cambridgeshire Constabulary (until June 1994) and Superintendent Bob Good of Essex Police (until June 1995). There was a scientist on the group and following much research and feedback from the public, the 'Battenberg' livery was recommended to the ACPO Traffic Committee who accepted it. In some forces there was some resistance, but eventually it found favour and is now used by the Ambulance and Fire Services as well as the police.

In July,1988 I was asked to chair a working group to prepare a response on behalf of the United Kingdom Police Service to the publication of the Road Traffic Law Review, chaired by Dr Peter North. It was published on 12 April and contained over 100 recommendations. It was the first major traffic review for many years. The secretary of our group was Chief Superintendent Frank Garratt from Warwickshire and we met three times in Sutton Coldfield. I suggested to the working group members that we should have a chat with Dr North. It was agreed and together with a Superintendent and the then Sergeant Alf Hitchcock from Lancashire, we went to Oxford and had a very interesting discussion with Dr North, a gentleman and true academic who was certainly au fait with his report.

It was very satisfying that ACPO Traffic committee accepted our report with the most minor amendments and forwarded it to the Secretary of State for Transport. Our working group members had real concerns about the offence of reckless driving. We discussed this at some length with Dr North, as we felt that the public understood what dangerous driving was but had difficulty with reckless driving. It was well put by Louise Butcher in the House of Commons Library Briefing Paper Number SN01496, 7 December 2016 in her background to the 1988 North Report.:

"The legal definition of recklessness in England and Wales, which was not defined in the Road Traffic Act 1972, was found to contain an element of subjectivity which was difficult to prove. The Review recommended that the offences of

reckless driving in the 1972 Act (later consolidated into the Road Traffic Act 1988) should be replaced by ones more firmly based on the actual standard of driving".

The Conservative Government's subsequent White Paper, published in 1989, considered reform of the drunk driver law a priority... Introducing the paper to the House the then Secretary of State for Transport, Paul Channon, said: We aim to ensure that the penalty matches the offence and that those who drive very badly are properly punished. The present reckless driving offence does not operate satisfactorily in England and Wales, and must be changed. At the moment drivers are escaping conviction, because the law turns on the driver's state of mind rather than the state of driving. The Government therefore propose to replace the reckless driving offence with a new offence of dangerous driving based more firmly on the observable standard of driving. This offence will have two ingredients: the standard of driving must fall far below that expected of a competent and careful driver, and the driver must carry a danger of physical injury or serious damage to property. The present offence of causing death by reckless driving will be replaced by a new offence of causing death by dangerous driving. The present lower level offence of careless driving will be retained...".

The working group members were very pleased with the Government's response.

In September of that year, I presented a paper on motorway policing to the Annual Superintendents' of England and Wales Conference at the Imperial Hotel, Blackpool. One of my recommendations was that consideration should be given to setting up a National Motorway Group. Motorways transcend force boundaries and the public should receive a consistent approach from the motorway police. Well, that certainly got picked up by the national media.

The Force decided to put on a Licensing Seminar which my Department had to organise. As the Chief Constable said in his 1989 Annual Report (page 30):

"There has been an increasing concern about rowdiness in public places and attention has been drawn to the behaviour of drunken youths in town centres. One of the 1989 Force Objectives was to combat this behaviour and to ensure that Lancashire towns did not become problem areas. Against this background the Force decided to bring together recognised experts in the field of alcohol abuse and members of the liquor licensing industry to enable interested parties to exchange points of view and develop a greater understanding of the problems associated with alcohol abuse.

A Licensing Seminar took place at Hutton Hall on Saturday 6 May and was addressed by senior police officers, members of the criminal justice system, doctors, sociologists and representatives of the brewing and advertising industries. An insight was gained into the many and varied issues associated with alcohol abuse and delegates were presented with a valuable overview of this complex subject in local, national and international context.

A booklet has since been produced which is a valuable reference for anybody who is concerned about alcohol abuse and will serve as a permanent reminder of a particularly useful and well received seminar."

I am so grateful to my team, and the success of the seminar was in no small part to their great organisational skills.

On 16 May 1989, I had an interesting trip. It had been arranged by one of my Inspectors, Mark Bartlett. The Conservative Party were looking at the possibility of using an airship at the Blackpool Conference. We travelled to Cardington and had a presentation which was interesting. Our hosts said words to the effect that 'we were ready to go up'. I must confess that I had no idea we were actually going airborne. Mark just smiled. He had arranged it but did not tell me in case I had said no. So up we went and I have to say it was a very interesting experience. Nothing actually came from that trip; there were problems, not least about the type of advert which could be displayed.

Superintendent Gary Price was in charge of Communications before John Mallalieu, and Gary was responsible for the new Communications Room which was opened by HRH The Prince of Wales on 6 July 1989. The Lieutenancy is responsible for the protocol and planning of the Royal Visits. Gary was on duty and gave an overview of the project to Prince Charles, I thought Mrs Price should be in the centre with the rest of the guests which included Councillors etc. Kathy was invited, I spoke to members of the Lieutenancy and said that I thought that Mrs Price should be in the building. I was told that Kathy was invited because I was Head of the Department. Mrs Price was 'given a spot' at the front of the people gathered outside, I still think to this day that she should have been inside. The Lieutenancy team were not being difficult; they followed the protocol as they did when The Queen visited the Duchy Estate. At lunch, the Chief Constable was on the top table but his wife was on a centre leg of the table.

The principal officer in the Lieutenancy Office was Bob Holme who was responsible to the Clerk to the Lieutenancy, the Chief Executive of Lancashire County Council and of course the Lord Lieutenant. Bob was very experienced and the consummate professional, he was a great support to me and we became good friends. In retirement, we would get together for meals with Bob and his wife Marie and my old boss Keith Brown and his wife Margaret. Sadly Bob died and Keith and I were asked by Marie to speak at his funeral; we still keep in touch with Marie, Keith and Margaret.

On 11 July 1989, I had a trip in a McAlpine helicopter. It was a demonstration flight because the Constabulary was looking at purchasing one. I do not like flying in helicopters (I had flown out to the gas rigs in the Irish Sea on 28 June 1986 with ACC Mander and Detective Chief Superintendent Norman Finnerty. We had no visibility, had to wear survival suits and it was so noisy). Three years on had not made me warm to helicopters.

Between 29 April and 9 May 1990 I went on a Traffic European Study Tour visiting, Belgium, Holland, Germany and Austria. It was most interesting to see how the different forces tried to combat road traffic accidents, again, the use of automatic equipment was evident

Between 22/24 October 1990, I had to attend Northumbria Police HQ for a Diving Contractors' Course. At the completion of the course, I was certified as the Diving Contractor for Lancashire Constabulary and under the Diving at Work Operations Regulations 1981, was responsible for the Lancashire Underwater Search Unit.

The Diving Operations at Work Regulations 1981 describe my legal duty and responsibilities:

Every diving contractor shall in respect of each diving operation:

appoint one or more diving supervisors in accordance with paragraph (3) to be in immediate control of the operation;

issue diving rules in accordance with Regulation 9 and Schedule 1 for regulating the conduct of all persons engaged in the diving operation;

provide a diving operations log book, which is to be maintained in accordance with Regulation 6, and shall keep it for at least two years after the date of the last entry in it;

ensure that all plant and equipment, including any plant and equipment required by Regulation 12, which is necessary for the safe conduct of the diving operation is available for immediate use;

not permit the use of compressed natural air as the breathing mixture in any diving operation at a depth exceeding 50 metres except where the use is for therapeutic purposes.

Every diving contractor shall so far as is reasonably practicable ensure that-

each diving operation is carried out from a suitable and safe place with the consent of any person having control of that place;

emergency services are available including in particular in the cases of diving-using saturation techniques, or at a depth exceeding 50 metres,

facilities for transferring the divers safely under a suitable pressure to a place where treatment can be given safely under pressure;

there are effective means of communication between the place at which operations are being or are to be carried out and persons having control of that place, and the emergency services.

'saturation techniques' means procedures by means of which a diver avoids repeated decompressions to atmospheric pressure by being continuously subjected to an ambient pressure greater than atmospheric pressure so that his body tissues and blood become saturated with the inert element of the breathing mixture.

Our Diving Unit was a top team. One of the jobs they had was to search the town centre drains prior to major political conferences. I remember in the early hours of one morning walking near the Winter Gardens when a figure popped up from a manhole. It was Sergeant Bill Pearce, the unit leader and diving supervisor. Despite having what some may say was the 'shitty' job of the Conference, he came out with a big smile and a cheery response. About half an hour later, I thought about where he had been working as he tucked into a full breakfast, enjoying his sausages!

We also had a compression chamber which was used for treating divers referred by medics. It was used quite often. For example in 1993 the chamber was used by eleven people following referrals. All were suffering from diving related illnesses and two others from the effects of smoke inhalation. Treatments in the Compression Chamber were made in liaison with the Royal Navy Surgeon Commanders of the Institute of Naval Medicine.

In 1990, I was appointed the organising secretary of a National Motorway Safety Campaign to be held in 1991. With Chief Inspector Tony Morley and members of my team I attended a meeting at the then General Accident Insurance Company at their headquarters in Perth. Senior members of General Accident were present as was Peter Joslin, Chief Constable of Warwickshire and Chairman of the ACPO Traffic Committee.

We were well prepared and gave a presentation which was well received. The General Manager later said that they would be the principal sponsors and they would give me a six figure budget. I told him that his company should retain the budget money and that we would use it as we went along. The company's public relations officer Mr Ray Andrews worked very closely with us, as can be imagined there was much work to be done.

It was the varied nature of my job which made it so interesting. We now move forward to 1 March 1990 when we visited Gallup in London. We wanted to arrange a survey of drivers to identify 'dangerous driver traits'. It was a most interesting meeting and I found it very disciplined. You could not ask any question unless approved by Gallup. However, they were able to frame a question to ascertain if drivers who 'offended' would drive in the same manner if they had their family in the car.

The answers were interesting and helped us to produce a profile of the driver most at risk. For example, research showed that most of us break the speed limit, one in five motorists lane hog or weave in and out of traffic; two out of five motorists have 'nodded off' when driving on motorways; 43% of motorists leave insufficient time for journeys; 57% of motorway drivers drive too fast; 25% drive too close. Frightening figures!

On 17 July 1991, the National Motorway Safety Campaign was launched at New Scotland Yard by Sir Malcolm Rifkind, Secretary of State for Transport. Unfortunately, whilst he was being interviewed by National TV, the interview was suddenly cut short because the crew were needed elsewhere.

The campaign ran from 18 July until 26 July to target drivers who put themselves and others a risk. A very professional and visually dramatic leaflet was produced which in effect created a profile of the driver most at risk. The 43 police forces of Great Britain and Northern Ireland participated, supported by other organisations and private companies.

In his 1991 Annual Report (pages 21/22), the Chief Constable wrote

"The campaign was organised by the Chairman of the Association of Chief Police Officers' Traffic Committee. The National Committee met regularly at Hutton and this Force provided the National Secretary, Chief Superintendent Jeffrey Meadows and the Secretariat... Research and Gallup polls identified five dangerous traits associated with motorway driving, lane hogging, driving too close, driving too fast for the conditions, driving when tired, and leaving too little time for the journey. The theme of the campaign was 'Don't put yourself at risk' and leaflets, posters and a video with voice-overs by Lancashire officers, were produced in support of the theme... The North West Regional Launch was at the Charnock Richard motorway service area. This

was attended by the television and stage celebrity Linda Lusardi, Public Relations Officer of General Accident Mr Ray Andrews and representatives of the region's police forces,

Throughout the campaign there was intensified patrolling of the motorway network. Displays were located at the three motorway service areas in the county and they were manned by motorway officers who were able to give advice.

Whilst it is appreciated that it is very difficult to change the attitude of drivers, it is hoped that the campaign will have gone some way to change driver behaviour for the better".

I was very proud of my team who responded to any challenge I gave them with skill and professionalism.

Between 8 and 11 October that year Blackpool hosted the Conservative Party Conference, it had been a busy year for many officers planning for that conference. I was based in Blackpool for that period.

On 12 October that year we became victims of crime. Our home was burgled and some jewellery was taken, including Kathy's engagement ring, which I had had to save up to buy. However, they did not take the gold orchids I had brought back from Singapore. It was not hallmarked!

We had just nipped out for an hour to visit friends. On return we found the patio door forced and a garden edging spade was stuck in the lawn. I sent Kathy next door to our neighbour's house and I took hold of the spade and went into the house to search. I was joined by friend and neighbour Terry; the burglar/s had fled.

It was an unsettling time and Kathy stayed up cleaning all her drawers out and placing any of her clothes the burglar may have touched into the washing machine. My clothes were simply re-arranged and placed back in my drawers! At one time Kathy even wanted to move. We stayed in our home but the following year Kathy completely redesigned it and the alterations cost more than the original price of our bungalow! I later learned that a man in jail admitted our burglary and it was 'written off'. Not a very satisfactory conclusion.

However, there were a couple of much nicer events later that year, on 26 October our second grandson Thomas James Meadows was born at 5.34am weighing in at 7lbs 9oz.

On 1 November Kathy's sister Rose was married to Harry – third time lucky for her! And a group of us joined them in Cyprus for their honeymoon.

Still dealing with Road Safety, on 4 December 1991, I gave a presentation at Preston Guild Hall on non-compliance with Chapter Eight of the government's official Traffic Signs Manual, which deals with road signing etc. Prior to the seminar my traffic management team had videoed bad examples of road signing or lack of appropriate signing. The audience comprised of contractors and representatives of the utilities and other interested professionals. The video was well received. I shared the platform with senior members of Lancashire County Surveyors' Department and a representative of The Health and Safety Authority. The latter speaker made the point that in some fatal accidents at the workplace or on the road, consideration could be given to corporate manslaughter if substantiated by the evidence. He certainly made the audience 'sit up'.

At 12.45am on Tuesday 21 July 1992, I received a call from Assistant Chief Constable Derek McNamara to say that rioting was taken place on Stoops Estate in Burnley. Local youths had been taunting the police and trying to entice them into an area and bottles filled with petrol had been thrown at the police cars. Some private cars had been set alight as had a barricade which the youths had set up.

I joined the ACC at Headquarters and we drove to Stoops Estate. The violence had finished but there were still officers on the scene. I spoke to some of my Support Unit Officers who had been called in to assist divisional officers to get their feedback. The national media saw for the first time, the protective clothing and gear which we had provided to our Support Unit Officers referred to by some as 'riot gear'. There were reports that some residents had watched the rioting on their garden deckchairs.

Sadly, much of the criminal activity was seen as copycat behaviour. During that summer there was considerable disorder throughout the county and the country.

In late August, we had a presentation at Police Headquarters from a local designer who ran a Vehicle Maintenance and Testing Consultancy. He had designed a full scale two dimensional replica of a Force Range Rover which he felt could be placed on motorways.

> *"In conjunction with the Transport Research Laboratory, a one day evaluation was undertaken on the M55 motorway of possible traffic calming effect it could have. Although the evaluation was of short duration the early indications are that vehicle speeds fell from 83mph to 72mph.*
>
> *At the request of the Transport Research Laboratory, in order to evaluate longer term effects, the replica vehicle is being deployed on the motorway on a regular basis during the winter months with a view to further scientifically controlled analysis".*
> (Chief Constable's Annual Report 1992 page 24)

We had organised a press call and of course, there was a great deal of interest. On 16 April, 1992 the *Evening Gazette* put the replica on the front page with banner headlines 'ELLO 'ELLO and I got a bit of stick from that.

The phrase 'Ello 'Ello, reappeared about seven months later on 8 November. The well-known TV personality and Journalist Alan Coren wrote an article headed *'Ello 'Ello, what's all this then* for the *Daily Express*. He referred to our replica Force Range Rover two dimensional model. He clearly enjoyed poking a bit of fun at us and to be honest it was a humorous article, although we were trying to tackle bad driving.

He concluded his article, writing, "The police will be run ragged. They will not know what has hit them. They will be beyond all coping. I give the brains behind all this Chief Superintendent Geoff (sic) Meadows, fair warning: you have sown the wind, and you will reap the whirlwind. You are about to be blown flat".

Quite soon after that article, I had to go to London to give a presentation on behalf of ACPO so I took the opportunity of using that occasion to reply to Coren stating:

"Well, in quoting from the Old Testament book of Hosea (Ch 8, v 7) it seems that Alan Coren had assumed the role of The Almighty. Any theologians amongst you will have immediately recognised that the text he chose to paraphrase was part of a pretty powerful reprimand the good Lord was delivering to the Israelites. Amongst other things, they had created from their gold and silver, false idols – all we were trying to do was to get motorists to slow down! So the Almighty, that's the real one, not Alan Coren was certainly disapproving of false gods. Well, we felt, the incorrect use of speed can be a false god to some motorists. I also felt that if Coren could paraphrase the good book, why not me? My reply was taken from the same book of Hosea, and to you all I say:

'Who is wise, and he shall understand these things? Prudent and he shall know them? For the ways of the Lancashire Constabulary are right and the just shall walk in them – but the transgressors shall fall therein'. (Hosea Ch 14, v 9)"

I do not know whether Alan Coren came across my comments.

We never actually got to use the model operationally. There were problems with the cost of any prototype.

For the presentation, I asked colleague David Jones if he could do a drawing depicting a god like character blowing down onto a humble Chief Superintendent. He replied that he would do the drawing which we could copy for a slide. However he replied, "Sir, I will have no trouble drawing God but it is beyond the talents of any artist living or dead to draw a humble Chief Superintendent". What a great quote and David subsequently became a Chief Superintendent. He may, of course, have been the first humble Chief Superintendent.

During September an experiment took place when live traffic and travel news was broadcast directly in the morning rush hour from a BBC Radio Lancashire reporter based in the Force Control Room. It was an initiative agreed by the Chief Constable and I had to meet with senior BBC Radio Lancashire staff to sort out the practicalities. The Control Room duty officer would liaise directly with the reporter. I must say that I had misgivings but the scheme worked well and was a valuable service to Lancashire's motorists.

1993 was another busy year with varied demands on the department. Much time was spent planning for the Conservative party Conference and Royal Visits. The Support Unit supported Divisional Officers when a major disturbance broke out at Wymott Prison and was deployed inside the prison to protect key areas. An emergency control was set up at Headquarters to provide resources and back-up to the incident commander. The Mounted Branch was on patrol around the perimeter of the prison. My role was in the emergency Control Room supporting the overall commander.

In December, we launched the traffic automatic camera in Preston. Connected to loops set in the carriageway, the cameras were activated if a vehicle went through a red light and two photographs of the offences were recorded.

Team work is essential in the police service as in other professions. A good example of this can be found in the 1993 Chief Constable's Annual report (page 30):

"During September, Chief Superintendent Meadows gave a presentation, on behalf of ACPO Traffic Committee to the Sixth Biennial Symposium at the Centre for Transport Studies, Salford University. The theme was 'Recent Developments and Research in Road Safety'.

Once again, administrative support was enlisted in the research of newspaper items, obtaining statistics from the Home Office and DOT, liaison with several agencies including TRL and PSDB with regard to research and evaluation papers, liaison with the Metropolitan Police regarding their use of enforcement technology, and the scanning of research documents and government papers.

Mr Meadows' presentation was much appreciated by delegates and organisers alike, and he has been asked to give the same presentation to the Parliamentary Advisory Committee on Transport Safety in London during March 1994".

In my Department, our motto was 'Failing to Plan, is Planning to Fail'. We checked and double checked our figures and we rehearsed the presentation, more than once. When you give such presentation, your Force is on show. I mention this because my presentations were not a 'one man show'. The support I received from the ladies in admin and my secretary and the officers I worked with was first class. Without that support, I could not have performed as I did.

On 18 January 1994, together with other regional traffic officers I travelled to Belfast to attend the North West Senior

Traffic Officers' Conference. We had an overnight stay at the Stormont Hotel, our colleagues in the Royal Ulster Constabulary were delighted that we had chosen to visit Northern Ireland. It was a successful conference and it also gave us an opportunity to see the problems facing our RUC colleagues when they gave us a tour of Belfast.

The PACTS seminar in London on 1 March 1994 went well and was another opportunity to focus people's minds on road safety.

We had our own D Day on 6 June when my Department became Uniform Operations Support. The Force had to respond to the changing legislation as a result of recommendations by Sir Patrick Sheehy who was appointed by the then Home Secretary Kenneth Clark to chair the Inquiry into Police Responsibilities and Rewards.

At paragraph six of the Foreword and principles to his 2011 *'Independent Review of Police Officer and Staff Remuneration and Conditions, Part 1 Report'*, Tom Winsor (later to become Her Majesty's Chief Inspector of Constabulary for England and Wales) commented:

> *"In 1993, Sir Patrick Sheehy – an industrialist – chaired the Inquiry into Police Responsibilities and Rewards. He produced proposals which provoked such severe opposition from police officers that the Government at the time decided that, since its higher priority was the reduction of crime, the most controversial of Sheehy's recommendations should not be implemented, although a number of important changes did follow".*

However, included in the changes was the setting up of Basic Command Units (BCU) usually headed mainly by a Superintendent. Blackpool and Blackburn had a Chief Superintendent and the Motorway BCU was led by a Chief Inspector. In my Department,

Superintendent Bernard Kershaw led Traffic Support, he was also my second-in-command. Superintendent Roy Hutchings led Operations Support and Superintendent John Mallalieu led Communications. I headed all the branches and had regular meetings with my three Superintendents.

Day to Day there was really little change for me other than to ensure we all worked to Force Policy.

Chief Inspector David Winnard, the officer in charge of the Traffic Management personnel was awarded a Winston Churchill Memorial Trust Fellowships. He travelled to Australia to see how the Australian Police approached the drink/driving problem and he produced a report for the Chief Constable. Mr Johnson called me in, he was holding a tome – David's report. He said, "He's one of yours isn't he," handing me this tome which must have been at least an inch thick. "Have a look at it, and give me some feedback". I thought, "Thank you David. You have had a nice trip now I've got to read this". It was a good report with some useful information which was no surprise, because David was a conscientious officer.

In late September we introduced the first automatic speed detection cameras in the Blackburn area. Vehicles travelling in excess of the speed limit passed through a beam which activated the camera and two photographs were taken. Because of precise markings on the road surface, it was possible to confirm the speed of the offending vehicle by examining the two photographs and measuring the number of lines passed. This was useful if the accuracy of the equipment was challenged. Our aim in using this equipment was to reduce the number of people killed and injured on the County roads. The location of the cameras, painted yellow was based on speed of the traffic and accident records. We publicised the use of this equipment to make the public aware and there were warning signs in the vicinity of the cameras. As technology advanced, new equipment was developed and there are still plenty of the 'yellow' cameras in evidence today.

One of the events I was involved with was the Lancashire Automobile Club's (LAC) Veteran and Vintage Car Run from Manchester. The event usually called at Headquarters before going to Blackpool where there was a parade on the middle walk. We provided a couple of mounted officers in their dress uniform to lead the parade. Barry Morris, Blackpool's Publicity Officer and his colleague Mike Chadwick and I used to attend the planning meetings with LAC members, David Taylor, Alwyn Davis, Mike Wood and Chris Lee. We made a positive contribution to the success of the event which was much appreciated by the LAC team, so much so that Barry and I were made Honorary Life Members of this prestigious club which was founded in 1902.

I had a very pleasant surprise when in the 1994 Queen's Birthday Honours I received the Queen's Police Medal for Distinguished Police Service. At that time you did not go to the Palace and I was offered three venues; County Hall, The Lord Lieutenant's Home, Dyneley Hall near Burnley or Force Headquarters. I opted for the latter and that proved to be a good choice. I was allowed 60 guests which included colleagues from the County Surveyor's Department, Colleagues from County Hall, the Fire Service and the Ambulance Service and of course Constabulary colleagues.

The Investiture took place at 12.15pm on Thursday 29 September by Sir Simon Towneley KCVO JP, the Lord Lieutenant of Lancashire. There was a brief introduction by the Lord Lieutenant after which The Clerk to the Lancashire Lieutenancy Mr G.A. Johnson read the citation. Sir Simon then presented me with the Queen's Police Medal. Sir Simon gave a brief address and then invited the guests to partake in refreshments. I had worked with Sir Simon many times in the planning and during Royal Visits. I always found him very helpful.

Kathy, Darren, Anne (my first daughter-in-law) and Benjamin and Thomas attended. There was a nice buffet and the Chief Constable presented me with a framed portrait on behalf of the Force. I had visited the Photographic Department to have a photo taken for the official programme. When that was done, Adrian, the Chief Photographer said, "let's have a bit of fun," and he had me posing. Little did I know he wanted a photo to which would be framed and presented to me.

Benjamin and Thomas visited the Mounted Department, sat on police horses, had a photograph with the Chief Constable and they were taken with Kathy and Anne to Blackpool in the Chief's jaguar. It was a wonderful and treasured occasion.

The portrait was hung on a wall facing the staircase. Benjamin and Thomas stayed with us on many weekends. On one such occasion we caught three-year-old Thomas on the staircase with his back facing the portrait having dropped his pyjama trouser giggling and saying, "Kiss my bum Grandpa". He was of course being encouraged by his six-year-old brother.

I was also a member of the 'M25 Controlled Motorways Pilot Scheme Liaison Group' which had the responsibility to evaluate all proposed speed detection equipment for use in the United Kingdom. This meant that Lancashire Constabulary, together with other operating Forces were engaged in pre-type approval procedures evaluating the new matrix system combined with speed cameras on motorway gantries. This was an interesting scheme because for the first time we were to introduce speed detection equipment which could discriminate between the lanes. The loops in the road also meant that the mandatory speed limits reacted to the weight of traffic. Simply put, if an even flow of traffic could be achieved then there would be less chance of areas of conflict.

The forces covering the M25 were represented together with Dr Steve Lewis of Home Office Police Scientific Development Branch and senior Highways Agency Engineers. The first meeting I attended resulted in a good half an hour discussion as to who should chair the meeting. The lead Highways Engineer suggested it should be me. (By default I became the lead for the 'police team'). I reminded the engineers that I had attended an earlier meeting in London on the 25 November 1993, when the Chairman and Secretary of ACPO Traffic Committee (both Chief Constables) met with the Highways engineers' team. It was agreed then that this was a Highways Agency initiative. At that Mike McKinnon took the chair, at times there were difficult moments and Steve Lewis was a great support to me. We did actually work well with the Highways Agency Team because everyone wanted to see a successful outcome. I attended the final testing on the M25 and to see the system 'come to life' was quite a sight.

There were two interesting acquisitions in 1994. Our Underwater Search Team was the first in the country to get their own custom-built boat to help with underwater searches. The six-and-a-half metre rigid inflatable boat, powered by twin 60hp outboard engines was built to Department of Transport specifications and complied with new police codes of practice, which allow it to operate up to 12 miles offshore. It had to be named to be registered. I asked the Chief if he had a name in mind and he told me to choose one. I decided on 'Rosa Gallica' the name of the red rose of the House of Lancaster.

The Chief Constable was very keen to have a Force Helicopter, Superintendent John Mallalieu headed the project team and was responsible for the day to day running of Lancashire's first Air Support Unit. A Eurocopter Twin Squirrel helicopter was purchased and was based at the British Aerospace factory at Warton. It had all the latest technology. The unit consisted of one Inspector, one Sergeant, seven Constables and three pilots. It was a great addition and improved our capacity to provide a potential life-saving service. On 17 November 1994, the helicopter was officially launched by Mrs Ruth Henig, Chairman of the Police Committee.

1995 was the year of my retirement and I was still as busy as ever. Between 1 and 3 February, I attended a Senior Officers Seminar at the Emergency Planning College at Easingwold in North Yorkshire. One of my duties was to sit on Promotion Board Panels. For five years I sat with Assistant Chief Constable Keith Brown as the Headquarters Chief Superintendent.

I decided to retire in June. The timing of your retirement is a very personal decision and I went into to see the Chief to inform him. I left a meeting of my officers because I wanted the Chief to know first, we had a chat and as I was leaving to go back to my meeting, the Chief said, "I've something to tell you. I will be two weeks behind you". I had no idea that he was retiring but that reinforced my view that it was the right time to go.

I actually retired on 13 July 1995. I was still working in the office when at about 4pm, my deputy Bernard Kershaw tapped me on my shoulder and said, "It's time to go boss," or words to that effect. My drive home that afternoon was not a happy experience. I was leaving the job I loved. That same night, I was hosting my retirement party at Headquarters. Bernard had organised it and the details went out in the form of an operational plan, a nice little touch. Phil Leese, son of our oldest friends Dot and Harold had a coach at the time and he laid on transport from Blackpool to Hutton. That meant our friends could travel safely but still get involved in the celebration. I made our friend John Bamber Coach Master General and he, wearing a Scottish Jimmy hat, made sure everyone got on board.

It was a good celebration and Derek McNamara, my colleague and friend acted as Master of Ceremonies and there were several presentations. The Chief gave a nice speech and I was seen off in style.

I was fortunate to work with Brian Johnson CBE QPM DL a first class Chief Constable and I was grateful to him for keeping me as head of uniform operations for over 10 years. It had been a privilege to head such a great department.

CHAPTER TWELVE
RETIREMENT

It has proved quite difficult writing this chapter. As I write in 2018, I have been retired for over 23 years. If you are still with me and not bored, I do not want to go on Ad infinitum, so I will summarise and cover different aspects which to some extent dictated how my retirement went.

Unbeknown to me, as a retirement present Kathy had booked us on a trip to the Far East visiting Singapore, Hong Kong, Thailand and Bali. That took place in October. It was a most enjoyable trip and it was nice to visit Singapore where I had visited when working on the 'Handless Corpse' murder. Afternoon Tea at the Raffles Hotel was rather special and we experienced the ultimate in service. The pop group, 'Take That' were in the restaurant at the time of our visit. Also enjoyable was having a Singapore Sling in Raffles' Long Bar, where you threw your peanut shells on the floor.

In January 1996, I was contacted by Mike McKinnon who had retired from the Highways Agency. He wanted me to be a part time 'law enforcement adviser' and join the team that was bidding for a large Road Safety Project in Turkey. The team felt confident they would secure the contract and the negotiations went on well into 1997 and from 19 to 24 May 2017, I spent 22 hours researching and producing a report for them, identifying road safety initiatives, which was well received. The contract was not won and I have to be honest I felt a sense of relief, I did not really want to go to Turkey!

Of course, I had no secretary so I had to think about getting a computer and familiarising myself with modern technology. All the typing and word processing was done for me at work. On 2 February 1996, my next door neighbour Terry and I each bought a Dell computer. The memory capacity was so small compared to today's computers.

In November 1996, having completed 15 months uniform acting sergeant duties Darren was promoted to uniform sergeant at Bolton K Division. It was GMP policy at that time to promote detectives into a uniform role. On arrival at Bolton, Darren was welcomed by a uniform Chief Inspector who informed him that he was pleased to have an inner city detective in uniform and commented that he was finding it difficult to get his own CID staff to take out their personal radios when they were out at a job. Darren worked at Bolton Division for almost twenty years in a variety of uniform supervisory roles.

In January 1997 I joined Blackpool South Rotary Club, Keith Gledhill had asked me the year before if I was interested and I was not interested at that time. Anyway I joined and within six months was Assistant Secretary, being made Secretary in July 1998. I was secretary for almost 10 years at different periods. I was President in the Rotary Year 2004/05 and again in 20016/17. The Rotary year runs from 1 July to 30 June. I enjoy my Rotary and for the last two or three years I have been Public Relations and Communications Officer and Club Webmaster. We made some nice new friends and we have enjoyed some nice social occasions as well as giving service to others.

Kathy and I took piano lessons when I retired with a local music teacher. We tended to do more talking than playing. Kathy progressed better than me and I finished the lessons on 1 May 1997. I then started to concentrate more on the computer.

On 4 October 1998, Kathy and I celebrated our 40th wedding anniversary and we had our celebrations the night before at South Shore Tennis Club, Midgeland Road, Blackpool, with relatives and friends attending. What was nice was that Darren and his pal Tony Fitzgerald, who together at the time performed as an Irish Folk duo played, 'I'll take you home again Kathleen'. It was so appropriate because Kathy (full name Kathleen) was 16 years old when I met her.

There is a saying, "The King is dead, long live the King". I experienced this just after I retired, I decided to give some talks on a couple of murders I was involved in and also a talk on some of the experiences I encountered, many of which were amusing. I contacted Headquarters to get access to some of the material which I had in a file, only to find out that it had been cleared out!

I contacted the Chief Constable, Mrs Pauline Clare (the UK's first female Chief Constable) and was very grateful to her for allowing me access to reports, photographs etc. I had made it clear that we would use the talks to raise money for worthy causes, I then contacted the *Lancashire Evening Post* and together with my friend John Bamber we were invited to their Broughton Print Headquarters where we were given much assistance to copy the photographs we wished to use.

John and I have performed many times, he was my technical man for the two murder talks I gave. On one occasion we were giving the 'Handless Corpse' talk in Accrington, a young man introduced himself at the end of the talk. He was the son of the 'Handless Corpse Case' trigger man Andy Maher. He told me that his Dad had been released from prison and was actually considering coming to the talk!

On 17 February 1999, I had a meeting at Keith Gledhill's office on Sycamore Industrial Estate, Blackpool. Also there was Arthur Gwilt, Senior Partner with John Potter & Harrison: Chartered Accountants of Blackpool. Apparently, the solicitor who was the Clerk to the Charity for the Foxton Dispensary, (Registered Charity No 224312) had died and they were struggling to find someone to take over. Keith was the Chairman of the Trust and Arthur was a Trustee.

I decided to take on the role and was supported by Arthur and another of Keith's friends, Eric Boardman, a chartered secretary who had been persuaded to become treasurer. This is a noble charity and my successor Robert Dunn, a member of Lytham Rotary created a website, www foxtoncharity.co.uk which gives a background to the charity. I ran the charity for approximately eight years working with the Trustees. Arthur, Eric and I spent many hours together in connection with the business of the charity and became good friends. It was interesting that Arthur resigned as Trustee when I finished and Eric was not far behind once he found a replacement.

Time wise, running the charity was quite demanding, Kathy used to come with me when I visited applicants. She did not go into the houses, but knew to come and knock after a certain time and 'rescue me', this was important because many of the females were often alone. I was very fortunate that Robert agreed to take over as Clerk to the Charity.

On Monday 15 November 1999, Kathy and I attend Bolton Town Hall in connection with Darren's Chief Constable's Gallantry Award. Anne also attended. The Chief Constable David Wilmot presented the award to Darren and his colleague Constable Masters for their courage and bravery when they detained a man who had threatened them with a firearm.

In his statement for court, Darren said, "The male walked up to my door and I saw him place his right hand into the left hand side of his jacket. He then produced a shiny silver handgun which he pointed into the open window directly at my face. The handgun was placed so near to my face that I moved my head backwards in order to focus on it. I saw that the barrel was not blocked and the male had his finger on the trigger. At this point the male was a foot distance from me and the hand gun approximately two inches from my face".

The weapon was examined by a police firearms expert and was a Bruni 8mm blank firing handgun with one round still in the chamber.

The citation read:

At 10.30pm on Friday 10th July 1998, Sergeant Meadows and Constable Masters were on mobile patrol in Bolton when they approached a man who was acting suspiciously. The man moved towards the vehicle, producing a handgun which he pointed at Sergeant Meadows before running towards the rear of the vehicle.

Sergeant Meadows and Constable Masters alighted from the van. The man faced the officers, pointed the gun at them and discharged it in their direction.

Believing he was about to re-load the gun, the officers ran at the man, who discharged the firearm at the officers for a second time. The officers grabbed hold of his arm, causing the weapon to discharge for a third time. Despite this the officers detained and arrested him.

The offender was charged with possession of a firearm with intent to cause fear of violence and was sentenced to 5½ years' imprisonment".

We were very proud of Darren and his colleague and thankful that they had not been injured.

Sadly, the following month on the run up to Christmas Darren dropped a bombshell. He and Ann were separating. That made for a miserable Christmas and on 2 January 2000 Darren moved in with us for a spell.

The Civic Trust decided to support the Macmillan Windmill Centre, Blackpool Victoria Hospital and pay for a 'quote' for the entrance wall. They organised a competition among members. My quote 'Caring for today and tomorrow' was accepted on 17 July and can be seen on the wall, on the right as you enter the centre. I have passed it many times. And the reason I pass it, is because I have had quite a few visits to the centre to see my oncologist.

If Darren dropped a bombshell at Christmas there was a bigger bombshell to contend with in 2001. I decided to have a PSA test (Prostate-Specific Antigen). This is a test which may indicate prostate cancer. It is indicative rather than diagnostic. However, it is the only available test. Following my test I was called into see Dr Garstang on 18 April. I had a quick referral and on 9 May was seen by Mr Bevis, Consultant Urologist. After an examination he said in a stentorian tone, "I think you may have an early prostate cancer. The good news is that if it is not aggressive, you can live for 10–15 years". At this point you are mentally trying to work out what age that would take you to. I was 61 years of age.

I was in BUPA so I arranged a quick biopsy which took place two days later on 11 May.
That night we were going to a Rotary Charter Dinner. I was sat down when our friend Colette took a flying leap and landed on my lap. That caused me to wince. I opted for the radical prostatectomy because at that time it was seen as a good option. If I needed radio therapy that could follow surgery, but you could not have surgery after radiotherapy.

There was a complication in that my surgeon was visiting the USA for a medical conference. He put me on some pills in the meantime which were meant to slow down any advancement of the disease. We went on holiday to Canada with John and Eileen Bamber returning on 1 June and from 10–15 June we went on a trip to the Black Forrest followed by a trip from 28 September to 4 October to Scarborough with Darren, Benjamin and Thomas.

After the surgery, which did not take place until 6 August, Mr Bevis said that they may not have got all the cancer out. I had so many hospital visitors; one day it was 18, another it was 22 and at one time I was not feeling too well. Barry and Colette Birch came to visit with two other friends. The nurse became concerned and said I needed a rest. Colette was in full flow and was still talking when Barry ushered her out. Barry's sense of humour is much like mine; when I was diagnosed, he asked me if I had any new shoes I hadn't worn!

That said, you have life and although I have never actually been free of the dreaded disease and have had regular urologists or oncologists appointments you get on with life. I am a great believer in positive thinking. (In 2012, I was required to have a five-week course of radiotherapy at the wonderful Rosemere Centre at Royal Preston Hospital and in 2017, I was on what I call the magic pills which lowered my PSA from 17 to 0.02 in about two months).

Christmas 2001 saw Beverley, Darren's partner spend her first Christmas with us. Beverley was a Constable of Greater Manchester Police. She was a front-line officer in Wigan Division and retired in 2016.

On 28 January 2002, Kathy went into Fylde Coast Hospital for partial removal of her thyroid. The surgeon was Mr Forrest who was very good. However, he had to sit on the bed to calm her down as her blood pressure was high. He was very kind and explained to her that he was very experienced in performing this operation. That did the trick and the surgery went ahead. She came home on 1 February.

In February 2003, Darren told us that he was buying a house on the A666, Blackburn Road, Egerton, next to Christ Church, Walmsley. It was a cottage with a slate roof. This was his first new house since he and Ann separated.

On 16 September I gave a talk to Poulton Probus Club, Bill Yates my old teacher was there as a guest of Tom Mayhew, another former Highfield teacher. It was when we were talking after the meeting that Bill suggested I write my memoirs, he said he would help. Sadly, I did not get cracking with it until later.

I had taken over as President of Blackpool South Rotary Club in July. It was Rotary International's Centenary in February 2005 so it was a busy year. On 25 February we had a Centenary Show and super buffet at the Grand Theatre. Paul Nicholas was starring in the musical show *Jekyll and Hyde*, he was photographed with Grand Theatre Director of Fundraising Elaine Fossett and me. We gave a cheque for £5,000 to help with renovations of a disabled toilet etc. Elaine and the General Manager Peter Cutchie were very supportive.

We did help to refurbish the disable suite and the well-known Rotary Wheel is engraved on the mirror in the suite. One way to raise funds was encouraging people to donate and 'buy' a seat. Because of our donation in addition to the 'Rotary Mirror', we were allocated a 'Blackpool South Rotary' seat.

It was my pleasure to induct Elaine into membership of our Rotary Club, as well as Orthopaedic Surgeon Steve Mannion (In 2008 he was described by the BBC as the 'Indiana Jones of Surgery' and appeared on BBC One's *'Super Doctors'* series alongside Lord Robert Winston). I also inducted into Honorary Membership of the Club, one time member of the Grumbleweeds, Theatrical Producer and Comedian, Tony Jo.

It is pleasing to report that two are still members of the Club, Elaine only resigning in August 2018 because she was relocating to North Yorkshire. Tony Jo has made a great contribution to the Club and has produced professional shows at Highfield Humanities College to raise funds for students to partake in Rotary Sponsored projects such as outward bound type courses, Rotary Young Writer, Young Photographer and Young Artist Competitions.

17 May 2006 was a good day. Darren and Beverley got married and Beverley became our daughter-in-law. She has been a

wonderful daughter-in-law. She is very caring and I think some of that has rubbed off on Darren. Darren is a good son, but I think he has become more thoughtful. Beverley is a treasured member of the family. (They sold their house in Leigh and moved to Poulton-le-Fylde in May 2018. Kathy and I think that they moved 'to keep an eye on us').

Rotarians are constantly being urged to raise the profile and awareness of Rotary, no better example of this can be found than the World Kite Flying attempt at the annual RIBI Conference in Bournemouth in April, 2007. It was proposed to fly 1,000 blue and gold kites bearing the Rotary logo to beat the current record of 672 in the Guinness Book of Records. They reached 927 but that record has been beaten. It was all about raising the profile

The Rotary Club of Blackpool South has been successful in raising the profile of Rotary through the various club projects and activities they have undertaken, I put one novel idea to our then Club President Keith Gledill. Keith was very much immersed in Rotary and was a Past District Governor. I suggested that the club could appoint its own Town Crier to publicise the club.

Blackpool is fortunate to have a high profile Town Crier, Barry McQueen. Barry, who is Vice-Chairman of the Loyal Company of Town Criers is also the Virgin Town Crier, and was before its demise, Boddingtons Brewery Town Crier. He is well-known and is often to be seen in the local media and on regional television. In his other role as Toastmaster and Piper, he has officiated at high profile events such as the weddings of international footballers, Michael Owen, Robbie Fowler and Jamie Carragher. Examples of his other duties include being Fanfare Trumpeter for Her Majesty The Queen, on the final day of her Golden Jubilee Tour and Fanfare Trumpeter at the G8 summit meeting in Birmingham.

With the approval of the President, I spoke to Barry who had said that he would be delighted to be the Town Crier for Blackpool South Rotary. On 5 March 2007, Barry was appointed the official

Town Crier for Blackpool South Rotary. In fact we take the view, notwithstanding there are other Town Criers who are Rotary members, none had been officially appointed for Rotary. Our claim is that Barry is in fact the world's first official Rotary Town Crier. No one has challenged that claim yet! Barry has been a great asset to the Club.

On 4 October 2007 we celebrated our 50th wedding anniversary with a very nice celebration with family and friends at the Carousel Hotel, Blackpool. That was followed by a nice weekend at the Swan Hotel at Newby Bridge, arranged by Darren and Beverley.

Our Rotary Club has a very good relationship with my old school Highfield. The former Deputy Headteacher, Peter Westhorpe created a Rotary Wall in the entrance of the new school which opened in 2012. Peter has been a great supporter of the club, even after he retired in 2015. This support was recognised by members and on 26 February 2018 he was inducted as an Honorary Member of Blackpool South Rotary.

Life has generally been very good, we have enjoyed good friends like Harold and Dottie Leese, John and Eileen Bamber; Marie and Gordon Bennett and Terry and Val Kennerley, and we made many good friends in Rotary. We had good holidays including some nice cruises to the Fjords, the Baltics, the Mediterranean and Adriatic Seas, the Caribbean and through the Panama Canal, but most of all we have enjoyed a very good family life.

We did have a caravan, as did Darren and Beverley on the same site in Newby Bridge in the Lake District National Park. We had the holiday home for about seven years and had some nice times meeting up with Darren and Beverley. I did not regret buying it and I had no regrets about selling the caravan. Darren and Beverley sold their caravan not long after we sold ours.

Our oldest Grandson Benjamin, 30 years old, graduated from Bolton University with a 2.1 Honours degree. He majored in history. He has made his own family with his partner Trilbie. They made us Great Grandparents with the birth of Dylan Lewis who was born on 27 April 2014, and Holly, our first girl in the family, who was born on 10 March 2016. On that day, we were at the funeral of a young friend, Mark Bennett who sadly died at the age of 49 years. His wife Sandra is a policewoman in Greater Manchester Police. Mark was a drummer in the group Echo, of which Darren was a member of. It was uncanny that as one life ended a new life was born.

Thomas our youngest grandson is 26 years old. He achieved excellent 'A' level results gaining an 'A' grade in graphic design and a 'B' grade in photography. He had no trouble in securing a university place. However, he did not settle and left university early. He became involved in the Scout movement and went through the Duke of Edinburgh (DofE) scheme reaching Silver standard. After a break he resumed the DofE programme achieving the Gold Standard Award, which amongst other things included some leading of an expedition. On 19 March 2018, he attended St James Palace where he received his certificate from TV Presenter, Adventurer, Explorer and Naturalist – Dwayne Fields FRGS. Also present was HRH The Prince Edward, Earl of Wessex. Thomas enjoyed his chat with Prince Edward. Thomas is an activity instructor with an outdoor pursuit company.

Darren retired from GMP in January 2016 in the rank of sergeant. Kathy, Beverley and myself attended his retirement ceremony at the Sir David Wilmot Suite, Sedgley Park. His name was called out and a senior officer gave a short history of Darren's service and commented:

> *"Darren has enjoyed every minute of a very good career in the police, picking up lots of awards along the way. He actually received six commendations in one five-year period. He was particular pleased to receive an award for Outstanding Leadership at the Bolton Division Excellence Awards, 26 years into his career, thus proving he still had*

the drive and commitment he started out with. In true cop fashion he played down a chief constables commendation for bravery in 1999 as (just) 'when we disarmed a male with a handgun'.

Darren then received his certificate of service from Chief Constable Ian Hopkins.

Big brother Jim died on Wednesday 20 January 2016, he was in a Nursing Home suffering from early vascular dementia but was very happy there. He had excellent family support from wife Sheila and his son Paul; Sheila's daughters' Karen, Beverley, Melanie and their families and of course friends. The last time brother Pat and I saw Jim was when we visited on the Wednesday previous to his death, he was very content and wished us "God Bless You" as we left. We are still in contact with Sheila and she has a very supportive family. He was very lucky because his daughters from his first marriage Julie, Sue, Charlotte and Sandra kept in touch. They all have their own families except Sue who is single. Sue is a most caring girl.

Brother John lives alone at the farmhouse near Garstang. His wife Agnes, 95 years of age was in a Nursing Home at Bamber Bridge. In the last 18 months or so she was often in a confused state, she died on 3 March 2018 and was buried on 17 March at St Helens, the family church at Churchtown. Demonstrating a copper's humour, Darren jokingly asked if he should bring his banjo as it was St Patrick's Day!

John has been diagnosed with early vascular dementia and carers call four times during the day. His daughter Elizabeth and her husband Will, live in a converted barn at the entrance to the farm. Their older son Simon is a gamekeeper and he lives with his partner Rebecca-Ann in Dalwhinnie, Scotland, with their three children. Younger Son Christopher is an outdoor activity instructor, when he is at home, Christopher helps out at nearby farms.

Brother Patrick lives alone in a flat in the north of Blackpool. He is very much involved in activities such a crown green bowling and as a former Club Concert Secretary, still keeps in touch with friends connected with that part of his life. He is still very friendly with his former partner Lynne and is close to her son Kevin. Patrick also had a son Michael from his first marriage. Sadly Michael died on 20 August 2018 after suffering from a fatal heart attack. He was 53 years of age. He was so popular that his many friends raised the money to give him a 'great send off'. There was standing room only at the funeral service.

Sister Joan spends much of her time with her family. She has a son Alan and daughter Lorraine who is married to Maurice. They have their children, and grandchildren which means that Joan has grandchildren and great grandchildren. Joan has a lovely family.

Kathy has a younger sister Rose who is married to Harry Beard. Rose has a son Grant and daughter Michelle. Grant has two daughters Tor and Charlotte and has a partner Kelly who has a young son. Michelle is married to Jim, who unfortunately suffers from ill-health. They have a son Robert, who has a lovely baby daughter Florence. Florence lives with her Mum Lexi but Robert and his parents see a lot of her.

Kathy and Rose's brother Brian lived on his own after he was divorced from Maureen. Sadly he died on 26 January 2018; he had been suffering from lung cancer. He had been discharged from hospital and died peacefully at home. His son Mark and partner Fiona gave Brian great support and Brian was very proud of Mark. Mark had worked in garages dealing with heavy goods vehicles. However, in his mid-twenties he went to Northumbria University to study building surveying, graduating with a first class honours degree and student of the year. He saw his dad off in good style when the funeral took place on 16 March. The chapel at the crematorium was full of Brian's friends from his beloved RAFA Club in Newton Aycliffe.

We have cousins who live in East Lancashire at Great Harwood, where my father was born, and in Accrington where my mother's sister settled with her family. Cousin Melvyn Howarth and his wife still live in Accrington, Melvyn and his sister Patricia are the surviving siblings of three children.

The Great Harwood matriarch, Dorothy passed away on Tuesday 20 March 2018. Another link with the past gone. Her two daughters Andrea and Nicola and their families still live in the Great Harwood area.

My late Uncle Patrick's family, the Horrocks and Denvirs live in the Ramsgate area. When we were youngsters we were visited by Uncle Pat and his young son Patrick, who we knew as Sonny. They cycled from Ramsgate to Whitehaven, calling off in Blackpool to see his sister Julia and her family.

We also have a cousin Geoff Dixon who lives in Egremont, near to my mother's birthplace of Whitehaven.

Cousin Raymond Taylor and his wife Margaret of the Great Harwood clan moved to New Zealand. Raymond died in New Zealand and his widow Margaret remained in New Zealand. Two of their children Tina and Lee and their families also moved to New Zealand, whilst their siblings Antoinette and Raymond and their families still live in the Great Harwood area.

The National Health Service comes in for a lot of stick. But up to now, I have been looked after very well, whether it is at the Blackpool Victoria Hospital, the Walk-in Centre Blackpool, the Rosemere Centre Preston, by my oncologists, urologists, nursing teams or by my local surgery. All have given good service with a special mention for the lovely Health Care Assistant Nicola at my surgery and my old practice nurse Bertha who is now my chiropodist.

I often think about people I have worked with and it is always nice to see lads you have worked with progress to high office. Three of the Inspectors who worked with me in Uniform Operations went on to become Chief Constables.

When Ian McPherson was a Support Unit Inspector I had to send him home because he was unwell. He had been suffering from a bad bout of flu. It was obvious to me that he had come back too early and he did not want to go home, he wanted to work but he did go home. He went on to become Chief Constable of Norfolk, later becoming Assistant Commissioner for Territorial Policing in London with the Metropolitan Police Service. He retired to pursue a career within the private sector in Canada and America.

Michael Barton was an Inspector in the Uniform Operations Planning Office. He was a bright lad and quite laid back. A proud Lancastrian, Michael was appointed Chief Constable of Durham Police in 2012. He still serves the people of Durham.

Of the quality of policing in his Force, their website proclaims: "Michael has introduced new ways of tackling organised criminals, using methods that challenge traditional policing and involve local beat officers and PCSOs, and encourage paradigm shifts.

"Durham is now recognised as a leading force in tackling serious and organised crime as well as managing offenders. A glance at the most recent HMIC PEEL inspection will show a police force at the top of its game with an enviable slew of outstanding grades. Michael attributes this to inspired and positive staff who have their feet on the ground and a burning desire to look after victims of crime and anti-social behaviour. The most often repeated phrase of visitors to Durham Constabulary is 'it feels different here'."

I first met Alfred Hitchcock not long after I took over Traffic and Uniform Ops. This young constable came into my office and I told him that he was being promoted to sergeant. He left the office with a big beam on his face. At various times Alf came back to work for me as Sergeant, Inspector and Chief Inspector.

It was clear that his lad was destined for high rank. After a while, I thought that Alf should go to a busy division for more experience. I contacted my pal Ken Mackay who was Divisional Commander at Blackpool and we arranged a swap.

Alf went to Blackpool and Chief Inspector Ian Bell came to me and took over Alf's duties in Traffic management and Technology. This introduced Ian to the speed cameras and he sat on the committees. He landed on his feet when he retired to become ACPO's Safety Camera Co-ordinator, which was a specialised role. At a lunch in December 2017, he jokingly thanked me for helping him to buy his bungalow in Spain.

Alf went on to become Chief Constable of Bedfordshire before moving to the MOD Police. Sadly he died in 2017 after a short illness aged 58 years. Throughout his life he retained his youthful looks.

The below tribute was published on the Government website:

"On Friday 16 June the sad and untimely death of Alf Hitchcock, the Chief Constable of the Ministry of Defence Police (MDP), was announced... In 2009, Alf was appointed Deputy Chief Constable at the National Policing Improvement Agency at Bramshill to help set up the new National College of Police Leadership and to review its leadership courses.

Alf was the national policing lead for equality and human rights for four years until 2016. He was also the national police spokesman on Knife Crime, and in 2008 he was appointed by the then Home Secretary, Jacqui Smith, to develop and lead the National Tackling Knives Action Programme.

Moving to Bedfordshire Police in 2011 as the Chief Constable, Alf led a complete restructuring of the force, which resulted in double the national average levels of crime reduction and similar improvements in detection of crimes across the county,

whilst meeting the budgetary challenges during this period. It was these skills and qualities that led to his appointment as the Chief Constable of the MDP in 2013..."
(Source: https://www.gov.uk/government/news/chief-constable-alfred-hitchcock)

Alf's death was a great loss to his wife Helen, his two daughters and their families and the Police Service lost a great leader and policeman.

I took great satisfaction from those who attained Chief Constable Rank, I was also delighted to note what Paul Brooks, one of my former motorway patrol officers had done in retirement. Paul is the Chairman, a founder and a Trustee for the charity, North West Blood Bikes – Lancs & Lakes.

On 4 July 2016, Paul and Blood Bike members attended County Hall to receive their Queen's Award for Voluntary Services from Lord Shuttleworth KG KCVO Lord Lieutenant of Lancashire. This award is equivalent to the MBE.

The Blood Bikers are volunteers who; *'ride motorcycles to collect and deliver urgently needed whole blood, platelets, samples for analysis, medication, patient notes, small medical instruments, donor breast milk, etc., between NHS hospitals without charging the hospitals'.*
(Source: www.nwbb-lancs.org).

I also have a great respect for friend and former colleague Stuart Sykes MBE. In 1978 whilst serving in Blackpool Division, with the approval of his senior officer, he started up a local youth group offering the Duke of Edinburgh Award Scheme (DofE). Stuart retired from the Lancashire Constabulary in 1989 and in retirement, through the Windmill Youth Group, he saw hundreds of young people through the DofE programme enriching their lives and deservedly received an MBE for his services to youth.

It is a small world; Stuart's wife Lesley is the niece of the late Alwyn Greenwood, my manager when I worked at the Harrowside Co-op Butcher's Shop.

I made reference in Chapter 8 to the tragic death of Superintendent Gerald Richardson GC. At the time of his death Gerry was an active member of the Rotary Club of Blackpool North and he was passionate about helping young people. He was held in great respect, not only in the Constabulary but in Rotary. To commemorate Gerry, his Rotary colleagues set up a registered charity, The Superintendent Gerald Richardson Memorial Youth Trust. The aim was to support any young person aged 25 years and under and who live or work within 15 miles of Blackpool Town Hall. The Trust gives grants, *'To promote youth development by supporting young people to attend courses and activities of an educational, cultural, sporting, adventuresome or character-building nature'*. This is a very wide remit but applicants do not get a full grant, they will if successful receive a percentage of the costs involved. They are encouraged to show how they themselves are raising some of the funds needed. Gerry's Trust was launched in 1974, and since then it has assisted over 17,000 young people and disbursed well over £280,000 in grants; a truly wonderful legacy.

We are indebted to the Rotarians who set up the Trust and particularly the Trustees who over the years have given great service to the Trust, i.e. Doug Leatham and his colleagues Charles Tyrell, Charles Merrill and Chris Holden and members of Blackpool North Rotary Club.

I was invited to join the committee in 2009 and I am on my fifth year as Chairman of the Trust. Gerry's widow Maureen is a Trustee. My colleague from Blackpool South Rotary, Jacqui Longden is also a Trustee. Jacqui was the Manager of the Blesma (The Limbless Charity) Home in Lytham Road, Blackpool. It closed in October 2016 after looking after limbless veterans for 67 years. It was pleasing to see that Jacqui was awarded the British Empire Medal in the 2017 Queen's Birthday Honours for her services to veterans. It was so very well deserved.

The Trustees are determined to do all they can to ensure that Gerry' legacy endures long into the future thus supporting young people. We have a hardworking secretary/treasurer in accountant David Williamson. We have varied experience with Peter Noblett, a former Rotarian and Chartered Surveyor; Kim Jackson a senior manager with Harry Ramsden's; Michael Gradwell, retired Detective Superintendent who has taken on the role of PR and Media Officer; Pauline Wigglesworth from Blackpool Council. In the last 12 months we have been delighted to add serving police officers to the Trust; Detective Chief Superintendent Sue Clark, head of Lancashire CID, Chief Inspector Lee Wilson in charge of policing the Blackpool area; Inspector Chris Hardy, Projects Officer, for the New West Division Police Headquarters on Clifton Road, Blackpool and Sergeant Gareth Tupman who is constructing a modern and appealing website for the Trust.

We have been fortunate that retired High Court Judge, Sir Richard Henriques has agreed to be patron. Joining him will be Professor Steve Finnigan CBE QPM DL (former Chief Constable of Lancashire Constabulary); Andy Rhodes QPM BA (Hons), Chief Constable of Lancashire Constabulary and Tony Jo, Theatrical Producer and Comedian. Our complete team gives us much confidence for the future of Gerry's Trust.

There is one annual event which the Trustees look forward to organising; the Special Schools Music Festival takes place in May. Pupils from the six special schools in Wyre, Blackpool and Fylde Boroughs participate. The pupils are from: Great Arley and Red Marsh schools in Thornton Cleveleys; Highfurlong, Woodlands School and Park Community Academy in Blackpool and Pear Tree School in Kirkham. These pupils are the stars of the Festival, for two hours they perform their music, song and dance acts. It is both humbling and inspirational.

Barry McQueen joins me and Ribby Hall characters Cyril the Squirrel and Dizzy the Duck to open the proceedings. I have even posed with Radio Waves chipmunks Chuck and Charlie! Barry plays the post horn gallop on his post horn and the children love it.

The event which is at Ribby Hall Village, Wrea Green is supported by the Mayoral Parties from all three boroughs and the Rotary's District Governor and spouse/partner.

There is usually over 100 children taking part and all receive a goody bag courtesy of Harry Ramsden's. The Harrison Family from Ribby Hall Village allow us to use their premises at no cost. In recent times, the Trustees have also organised two major Commemoration Dinners. The first one was on 23 August 2011 on the 40th Anniversary of Gerry's death. It was held at The Sponsors Lounge, Blackpool Football Club.

Tony Jo was Master of Ceremonies, a duty which he performed professionally and without charge. Our guest speaker was Mr Justice Henriques who gave a most interesting and enjoyable speech. When I spoke to Sir Richard to invite him to be the guest speaker, there was no hesitation and he said that it would be an honour and privilege to do it. There were over 200 guests, the Chairman and Secretary of the local branch of the National Association of Retired Police Officers (NARPO) Christine and John Pickard excelled and organised eight tables of 10.

Five years later, on the same date the Trustees organised a similar dinner, this time at the Imperial Hotel, Blackpool. Tony Jo again was Master of Ceremonies and as for the last dinner, he arranged the entertainment. Our Guest Speaker was former Blackpool Officer Mike Barton, now Chief Constable of Durham Police, Mike was very well received and was a popular choice of speaker. Our guests were Chief Constable of Lancashire, Steve Finnigan, his wife Jackie and Mike's wife Maggie.

These events are important to keep Gerry's Trust in the public eye and they also generated funds for the Trust. The Trustees intend to have more fundraising events. At the 2011 event, I gave the vote of thanks to Mr Justice Henriques. I also took the opportunity to pay my own tribute to Gerry referring to a saying attributed to Mahatma Gandhi which could have been written just for Gerry:

"I shall pass through this world but once. Any good therefore that I can do or any kindness that I can show to any human being, let me do it now. Let me not defer or neglect it, for I shall not pass this way again".

What better epitaph for this outstanding young Police Officer and committed Rotarian.

Having worked with Gerry Richardson I am sure that he would be so proud of what his Trust is achieving.

CONCLUSION

In an appraisal from the late Detective Superintendent Norman Finnerty, he wrote of me, "He does not suffer fools gladly. There are no frills with his dismissal".

In a briefing sheet for the Chief Constable for my retirement function, my second in command, Superintendent Bernard Kershaw wrote of me, "He is also a caring officer, despite the wide range of his responsibilities, the welfare of his staff is always paramount – and difficult as it may seem – in a quiet unobtrusive way he would make sure, often through personal visits, that all was well".

When you embark on a project such as writing a book, particularly about yourself it makes you think about how others see you. One sometimes hears the quote, "I am a self-made man," I do not subscribe to that view. We all need support at some time and I am extremely grateful to those who have supported me.

I always wanted to be a Bobby when I was young and to achieve your ambition is something not everyone can aspire to. When I joined Blackpool County Borough Police Force, I never dreamed that I could reach a senior rank. In fact, I think it is true to say that I achieved my ambition on 5 October 1957 when I became a Constable.

One thing that life teaches you is that you do not have all the answers. If I needed reminding of that, I had a constant reminder with a framed quotation on my desk. It was by respected military man and writer General Sir John Winthrop Hackett, GCB, CBE, DSO & Bar, MC. Sir John was the speaker at the Eleventh Frank Newsham Memorial Lecture on 29 July 1976 at Bramshill House. He said, *"There are flaws in anything man-made; nothing from the hand or mind of a man is perfect; even when you – a man too – cannot say how you improve it"*.

One thing I could not abide is members of the 'shudder brigade'. These characters appeared after someone had made a decision, often under trying circumstances. Then it started, "they should have done this or should have done that". These comments were quite often made by those who were not present at the time or who did not fully appreciate all the circumstances. What they do not seem to understand is that retrospective wisdom is a quality which by its very nature eludes those that have to make pressing or instant decisions.

If I had to give a short summary about my career, I can do no better than reproducing the back cover of the official programme for my Investiture of the QPM

"CHIEF SUPERINTENDENT JEFFREY MEADOWS, Q.P.M., B.A

Mr Meadows joined the Blackpool County Borough Police Force in October 1957. Following five years on beat patrol he transferred to CID duties. In April 1969, as a result of force amalgamations, he became a member of the Lancashire Constabulary.

Promoted to Sergeant in 1969 and Inspector in 1974 he performed both uniform section and crime patrol duties and detective duties in the Blackpool CID and Regional Crime Squad. He was promoted to Detective Chief Inspector in July 1978 and was appointed deputy head of the No. 1 Area Crime Squad. During the next four years he was involved in the investigation of serious crimes throughout the county, e.g. the activities of Chinese triads, the handless corpse case and the murder of Judge Openshaw. In October 1982, promotion to Superintendent came and he was posted to the Discipline and Complaints Department as an investigator, followed by a period as Sub-Divisional Commander at Blackpool South.

He was promoted to Chief Superintendent in March 1985 and heads the Uniform Operations Support Department (formerly Traffic and Uniform Operations). Mr Meadows is responsible for the co-ordination of all police planning for major events of a non-criminal nature, e.g. royal visits and government conferences etc. His department is responsible for all force-wide contingency planning, traffic and uniform policy and he commands uniform specialist groups including the Mounted Branch, Force Support Unit, Traffic Support Group, Support Services and Force Communications. He is Diving Contractor for the Underwater Search Unit. He is a member of several regional and national committees, e.g. the ACPO Police Regional Emergency Planning Committee No. 1 Region , The North West Senior Traffic Officers' Conference, the ACPO Standing Sub-Committee on Road Traffic Enforcement Technology and the M25 Controlled Motorways Pilot Scheme Liaison Group Meeting . He is also Chairman of the National Motorway Conference, a Sub-Committee of the ACPO Traffic Committee".

Kathy and I were married on 4 October 1958 and we had a most wonderful party at Blackpool Golf Club on 6 October 2018 to celebrate our Diamond Wedding anniversary. The golf club provided a sumptuous buffet for our 80 guests and Tony Jo took charge and ran the night. The entertainer was a young lad called Dan Chettoe who did a remarkable performance of Bring Him Home from *Les Miserables*. Darren and myself were the mystery artists and our enthusiastic performance of the Bold Gendarmes was well received by our guests.

I have so much to be thankful for; great support from my family and friends and work colleagues.

One thing you do learn in life is that every now and then life throws out a challenge. My latest challenge was received on Tuesday 6 November 2018. I had a meeting with my Consultant Urologist. He told me that the prostate cancer had moved into my spine. Apparently what usually happens is that the cancer compresses the spine and it could damage the spinal cord.

However, the injections I am currently having, have brought the prostate cancer readings down to virtually zero which meant that they did not think anything needed to be done at this stage And they would monitor it. I thought well I can deal with that.

I said, "And what else"?

Mr Ahmed and Clinical Nurse Specialist looked at one another. They had the result from my bladder examination. Mr Ahmed told me that I had an unrelated cancerous tumour in my bladder. So in addition to prostate cancer, I now had bladder cancer.

Their approach was very caring and took time to explain and answer and by the way, the bladder cancer is a rare one! My son Darren, a retired police sergeant was not shy of asking questions. There will be a Multi-disciplinary team meeting soon and from that will be a treatment plan, Melanie has looked after me since I was first diagnosed in 2001, she is great nurse and an excellent ambassador for the National Health Service.

I am a very positive person and my wife and family knows this. We will get on with life and live it as normal as possible. I have had great support from so many people. Thank you.

Now you might think that the title of my book is an odd choice. However, as I wrote earlier, that is what I was once described as. It is for the reader to decide if I was a *'Chief Constable's Nightmare'*.

Whatever decision is reached, one thing cannot be denied, this lad did not do too badly for a former Co-op butcher's lad!

A TRIBUTE TO MY FATHER, JOHN MEADOWS SENIOR

The Harwood Lad – A late casualty of War

From a mill town called Great Harwood he left to seek his fame.
At sixteen years, a willing lad but no money to his name.
He came upon a seaside town made famous by its tower.
Soon working on the railway, from hard work he'd never cower.

In later years the war clouds grew and a call to arms went out.
Young men responded valiantly the enemy to rout.
The Harwood lad traded railway clothes for a tunic and a gun.
To clear the skies, with his ack-ack gun, of the raging fighting Hun.

Across the globe the conflict spread with yet another foe.
To dangers new the lads were sent, to a land they didn't know.
Here pestilence and humid heat were unseen enemies to defeat.
And the steamy jungles took their toll, as in the night his breath they stole.

Six months before the end of war the news came in the mail.
The Harwood lad had been struck down but lived to tell the tale.
In Burma's hostile jungle, a leg wound he received.
But fate was on his side that day, his life would be reprieved.

From golden sands to jungles green the lads were sent to fight.
To witness horrors unforeseen – to put the Japs to flight.
Some died in lands so far away.
As they strove to keep the foe at bay.
But the lad from Harwood he came home.
Health broken down no more to roam.

The price he paid his breath they took.
Four medals in exchange and a discharge book.

His family he returned to, a bitter wiser soul.
To re-adjust, new things to do – and try to avoid the dole.
With the end of war came liberty, but the Harwood lad faced poverty.
No hero's welcome on return, must find a job so he can earn.

Labourer, baker, bin man, any job he'd try.
Money short thro' time off sick, hard times he would defy.
The children needed clothing – life was just a pain.
And the handout from the local police just added to his shame.

He lived to see his children grow and leave the family nest.
Unfit for work thro' failing health he'd given of his best.
Two decades after Burma, his breath he drew no more.
For the Harwood lad was really a late casualty of war.

ROYAL VISITS

1985

30 May	HRH Duke of Edinburgh visits Blackburn.
2 September	HRH Princess Alexandra.
13 December	HRH Duchess of Kent.

1986

12 April	HRH Princess Margaret at Poachers Inn, Bamber Bridge.
23 April	HRH The Prince of Wales and HRH The Princess of Wales visits Burnley, Leeds/Liverpool Canal, Queen's Mill and the Princess visited three schools for mentally handicapped children. They then went to Skelmersdale and Wigan.
9 May	HRH Princess Alice visits BLESMA.
27 May	HRH Princess Anne at Salmesbury.
4 July	HRH Princess Margaret at Preston and Blackburn.
20 October	President Mário Soares of Portugal visits Lancaster to celebrate the 600th anniversary of the Treaty of Windsor which exists between this country and Portugal. He visited Lancaster Town Hall and the Castle before being awarded an honorary degree in a ceremony at the university.
4 November	HRH Duke of Kent visits British Aerospace.
10 November	HRH Princess Anne visits Thwaites Brewery.

1987

7 April	HRH Princess Alice.
19 June	HRH Duke of Gloucester visits Rossall.

17 September HRH Princess Alexandra.
12 November HM Queen Elizabeth II.

1988

9 May   Her Royal Highness The Princess Anne, Princess Royal visits Regimental Museum at Preston.
10 May   HRH Duchess of Kent visits Beaumont College, Lancaster.
2 June   HRH Prince of Wales to Blackburn.
4–6 July   HRH Princess Alexandra at Lancaster University Graduation Ceremonies.
25 November   HRH Duchess of Kent visits Warton.

1989

7 March   HRH Princess of Wales visits Nelson where she attended the Help the Aged Resource Centre and the Ithaad Community Centre.
3 May   HRH Princess Alexandra to Bleasdale House, Silverdale, the YWCA at Blackburn and the Red Cross at Preston.
6 June   HRH Princess Alice opened the new Fylde Hospital in Pershore Road, St Annes and visited BLESMA in Blackpool.
1 July   His Royal Highness The Prince Edward visits the Helmshore Textile Museum, the Grand Theatre at Blackpool where he attended a performance of *Joseph and his Technicolor Dreamcoat* and later he was guest of honour at the Midsummer Ball at Rossall School, Fleetwood.
6 July   HRH Prince of Wales visits the White Cross Industrial Estate in Lancaster. Later he went to Roman Road estate in Blackburn, the Wolstenholme Rink Factory in Darwen and the South Ribble Enterprise Park at Walton-le-Dale. He then arrived at police headquarters where he opened the new Communications Centre.

12 July	HRH Princess Alexandra visits Lancaster University for Swan Lake Ballet.
27 July	HRH Princess Alexandra.
7 August	HM Queen Elizabeth II and HRH Duke of Edingburgh visits Duchy Estate in Dunsop Bridge and the Whitewell area.
15 November	HRH Duke of Kent visits two factories at Poulton-le-Fylde and Blackburn.
1 December	Her Royal Highness The Princess Anne, Princess Royal visits Wymott Prison.
6 December	HRH Princess Alexandra visits St John's Hospice at Slyne.

1990

18 April	HRH Princess of Wales visits Hutton for the ACPO Drugs Conference. She later went to GEC/Alsthom Traction Ltd in Preston before visiting Riversway Dock Control Centre and Tavern Furnishings Limited both part of the new development at Preston Docks.
9 July	HM Queen Elizabeth II visits Weeton Barracks to present colours to the First Battalion of the Queen's Lancashire Regiment.
12 July	HRH Princess Alexandra visits Lancaster University in her capacity as Chancellor to present degrees. Later in the month in her role as Colonel in Chief of the King's Own Border Regiment, she officially opened Alexandra Barracks at Lancaster.
9 August	HRH Duke of Edinburgh visits shirt manufacturers Stephens Brothers in Bispham.
12 September	HRH Duchess of Gloucester visits Lancaster to officially open 'Danish Week' events.
18 October	HM Queen Elizabeth II visits Clitheroe Royal Grammar School and Stonyhurst College, Hurst Green where she presented a new Guidon to the Duke of Lancaster's Own Yeomanry..

23 November HRH Princess Alexandra visits Royal Lancaster Infirmary to officially open the new scanner unit. The following month the final Royal Visit of the Year was made by Princess Alexandra when she again presented Degrees at Lancaster University.

1991

9 April HRH Princess Margaret visited the NSPCC Child Protection Unit at Wellington Street, Blackburn.

4 May HRH The Princess Anne, Princess Royal visited the Winter Gardens, Blackpool to attend the National Federation of Young Farmers' Clubs' Annual General Meeting.

7 June HRH Prince of Wales visits Burtonwood near Lancaster, Foxhill Bank, Accrington, Cuerden Valley Park, Bamber Bridge and Mere Sands, Rufford. All were connected with the Lancashire Trust for Nature Conservation.

2 July HRH The Princess of Wales visited Lyons Bakeries, the Streetlife Trust, Blackpool Town Hall and the Blackpool and Fylde Society for the Blind.

2 October HRH Duchess of York visited the Carr-Gom Society, Fulwood and Richardson House, Billinge End Road, Blackburn.

In November as patron of the Motor Neurone Disease Association the Duchess of York visited Preston Royal Hospital, Fulwood and Blackburn.

19 November HRH The Princess Anne, Princess Royal visits the Citizens Advice Bureau at Whitworth. In the same month The Princess Royal visited the Save the Children Fund, Cannon Street, Preston and the Conference of Occupational Therapists at Wellington Park Masonic Lodge, Leyland.

December The final Royal Visit of the year was made by Princess Alexandra when she presented degrees at Lancaster University and also opened the new Lancaster House Hotel in the university grounds.

1992

9 May	HRH The Prince Edward attended the 50th Anniversary of The Lancashire Council for Voluntary Youth Services at the Constabulary Training School at Hutton.
28 July	HRH The Princess of Wales visited four venues in Blackpool; the British Deaf Association Triennial Congress at the Winter Gardens, Tower World, The Fylde and Wyre Relate Centre in Clifton Street and Trinity Hospice on Low Moor Road.
July	HRH Princess Alexandra in her capacity as Chancellor visited Lancaster University to award degrees. She returned in December and in addition to attending the degree ceremony she opened Waddell Hall of Residence at St Martin's College.
December	HRH The Duke of Kent toured the Military Aircraft Division of British Aerospace within Warton Aerodrome and also visited Karrimor International Ltd at Accrington.

1993

13 January	HRH The Princess of Wales.
24 April	HRH The Princess Anne, Princess Royal visits Young Farmers at the Winter Gardens.
7 June	HRH The Prince of Wales visits Lancaster and North Yorkshire.

1994

9 February	HRH The Duke of Kent visits Eurava, Karrimor and Stringers.
11 May	HRH The Duke of Gloucester visited Fylde Farm and Preesall.
16 May	HRH The Princess Anne, Princess Royal visits Clayton Le Moors.

13 July   HRH The Duke of York visits Lancashire Fire and Rescue HQ.
22 July   HM Queen Elizabeth II visits Rossall School and Blackpool.
29 November   HRH The Duke of Gloucester.

Sister Joan's 70th Party - 14th December 2014

JOINT LANCASHIRE/CUMBRIA UNDERWATER SEARCH UNIT

P.C. 614 J. O'Hare, P.C. 491 S. Carruthers, P.C. 1167 P.Q. Harrison, P.C. 2933 K. Wilson, P.C. 643 G. J. Plummer, P.C. 245 A. Marshall.
P.S. 2008 W. H. Pearce (Senior Diving Supervisor), Chief Superintendent J. Meadows, B.A., (Diving Contractor), Superintendent R. Hutchings (Deputy Diving Contractor), P.C. 1205 J. Howard.

Under Water Search Unit Team

Jeff gets the Sharpe picture

Retirement coach

Jeff Evening Gazette

Darren and Jeff Bruche 1986

Tony Jo, Elaine Fosset and Jeff

Grand Theatre

Highfield School - Rotary Wall

Grand Theatre Seat plaque

Ben, Trilbie, Dylan and Holly

Steve Mannion Iraia Jaya

Ben at Graduation

Darren and Beverley just married

Darren and Beverley's wedding

Superintendant Gerry Richardson

Sir Richard & Lady Henriques

Chief Constable Mike Barton Durham Constabulary

Kathy, Rose, Brian and Mark

The Old Gang

Foxton Trustees

Darren with Flash

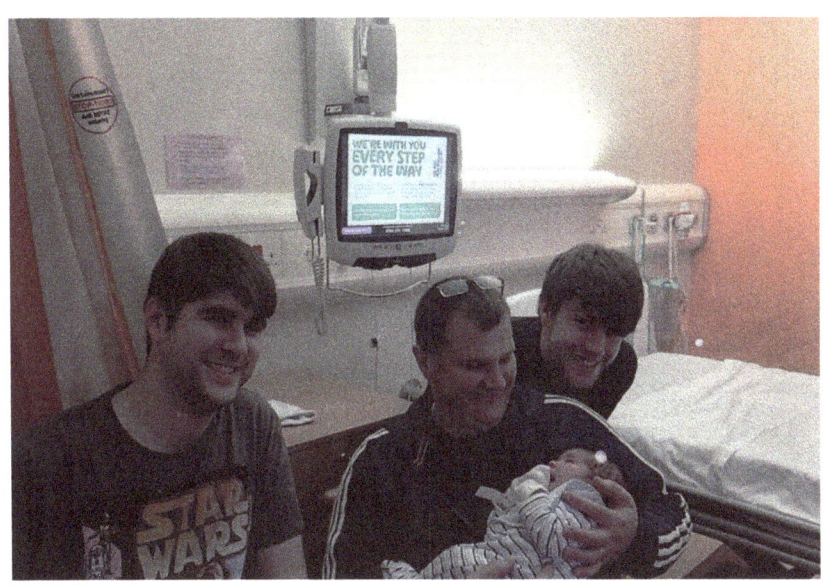

Darren, Ben and Thomas with Dylan

Chief Superintendent Jeff Meadows QPM

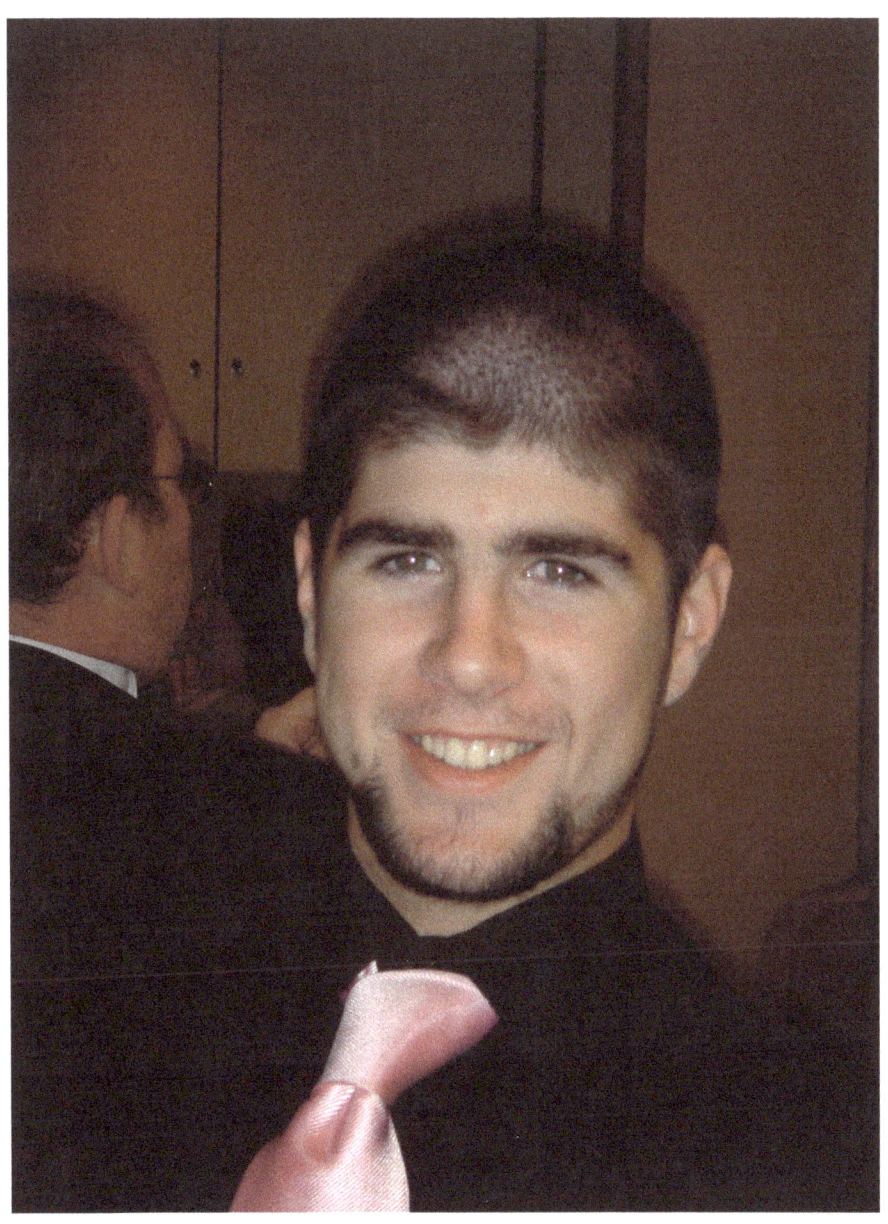
Ben August 2006

Ben 2018

Darren's graduation

Kathy, Jeff and the boys

Dear Jeff,
I am very sorry but I won't be at home this afternoon. I will explain it to you when I see you later on. (I have to work) Please will you meet me at half past five outside our shope or if you feel shy outside Jay's which is next door. I hope you don't mind, mind you I knew you will, but there is no harm in saying it. But please don't be mad when you meet me, or I shall sulk all night (which is unusual) haha. Anyway, I can't think of anything else to say. But keep your hair on.

All my love
Katie
x x x x

P.S. I love you with all my heart
x x x x x x

Spelt it wrong
I will try again ~~xxxxxxx~~ did it

Jeff is the one I love.
As if sent from above.
I only ~~~~
Jeffrey I am in love with you.
Kathleen

Kathy's Letter

PC Jeff Meadows

Rose, Brian and Kathy

Rose, Lucy and Kathy

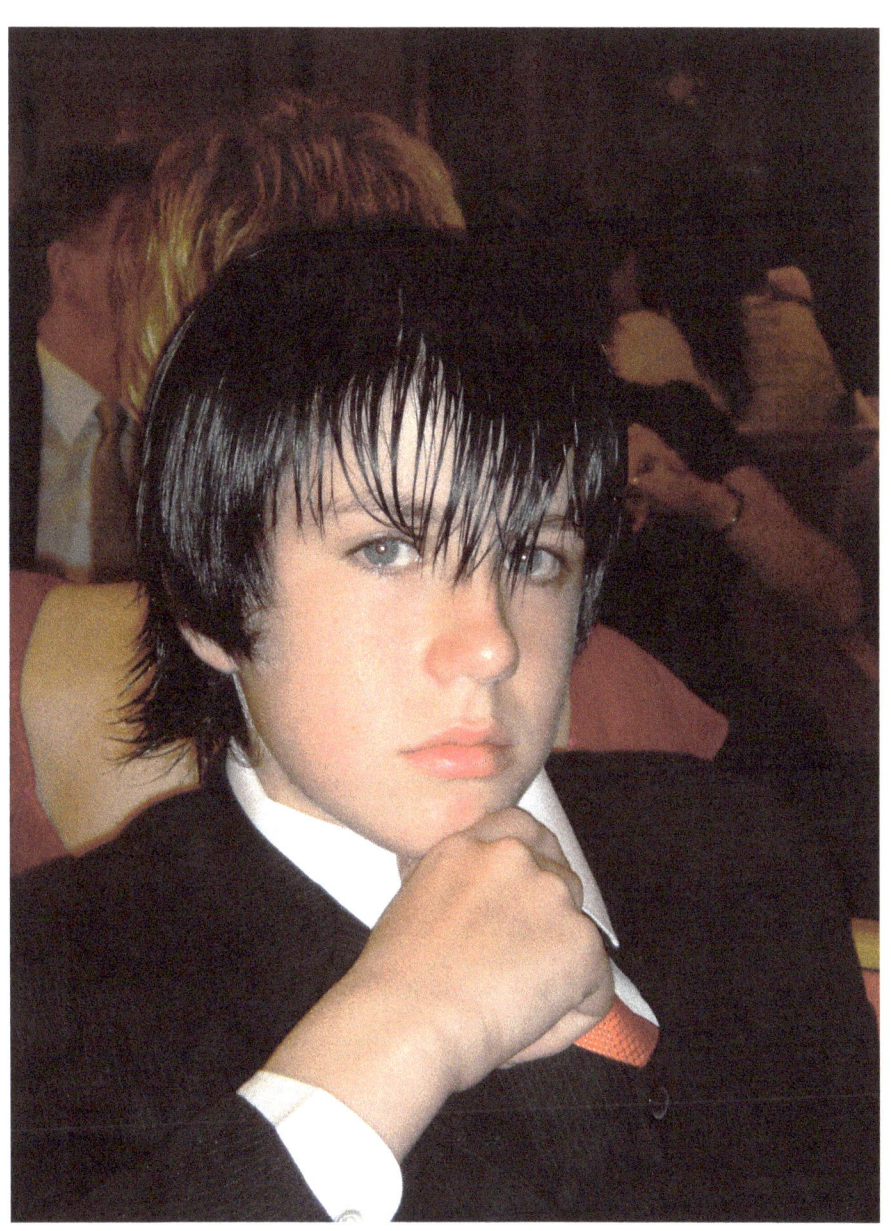

Thomas August 2006

Thomas Scouting

Thomas in Wales

Jeffrey Meadows QPM
15/07/1938 - 26/11/2018

www.ingramcontent.com/pod-product-compliance
Lightning Source LLC
Chambersburg PA
CBHW040317170426
43197CB00021B/2945